CONTENTS

WHAT TO EXPECT FROM THIS GUIDE

For each poem you'll find:

- The poem itself
- Context to help explore the poem
- Stanza by stanza annotation of thematic interpretation and language analysis
- Additional analysis of structure and form
- Key connections (theme and motif) with the rest of the collection

The analysis of poems is useful for either A or A-Level – they are standalone, but I make reference to the contexts and critical interpretations that are essential for A Level comparative questions.

You won't find a single, straight-forward interpretation – I don't believe that Rossetti's writing lends itself to such! Instead, I think Rossetti is often writing consciously, and there are several obvious themes. I also think there's some themes where we have to question how consciously Rossetti herself is exploring ideas – but that doesn't mean that they aren't present. Rossetti's poetry, for me, is full of doubt and religious conviction, complex considerations of women's rights and independent thinking, and a difficult relationship with sexuality. How much of that was in Rossetti's mind, I have no way of knowing – but as an A-Level student, one of the best things you can do is search for the complexity of meaning and acknowledge that literature speaks to different people of different things – even the writers themselves.

ABOUT THE AUTHOR

I've been teaching English Literature and English Language for more than seven years in my job as Faculty Leader at one of the top performing state schools in the North of England. We've been doing the new OCR spec, and I love the Rossetti collection they've included! She's a fantastic poet, with an incredibly depth which you don't always see at first glance – she's famous for a handful of poems popular at weddings and funerals, and the carol *It Came Upon A Midnight Clear*. But once you look into it there's just so much to explore, and my hope for this guide is that it gives you the confidence to understand the poems, and to form your own opinions and judgments as well.

By writing mini-essays of analysis, rather than labelling sections, I'm also showing you what I think good analytical writing looks like; not over-laden with terminology when it's not useful, but using a precise and detailed interpretive style. I'm happy to answer questions on my blog at www.charlotteunsworth.com, or through Twitter: @miss_tiggr

WHAT ARE ASSESSMENT OBJECTIVES, AND HOW DO YOU MEET THEM?

At AS-Level, this question's marked out of 30 on Shakespeare and pre-1900 poetry (Paper 2, section 2))

At A-Level, this question's marked out of 30, on Drama and Poetry pre-1900 (Paper 2, section 2)

Understanding the AOs: whenever I've attended examiner training with OCR they have been keen to stress that they take a *holistic* approach to marking. That means they identify where in the descriptors your essay is – Excellent, Good, Competent, Some, Limited – and then they use the assessment objectives to 'shade' the mark. So, for example, if you have an "Excellent" (top band) essay but you haven't fully addressed the dominant assessment objective, you'll be towards the bottom of the band. I have put below a breakdown of marks – so 50% is 15/30 marks for example – but this is more for you to practice and self-assess to check that you've hit the AOs enough, rather than to think "right, I've got 15/15 and 3/7". If the dominant AO is AO3, then your essay needs to focus on that – see "addressing the assessment objectives" later in this guide.

AO	AS-Level	A—Level
AO1: Articulate informed, personal and creative responses in literary texts, using associated concepts and terminology and coherent, accurate written expression	30%, 9 marks	12.5%, 3.5 marks
Can you write an expressive, detailed and well organised essay? Have you got something interesting to say that you confidently understand the poetry? Can you use literary vocabulary confidently, appropriately and selectively? Is your writing always accurate and developed?		
AO2: Analyse ways in which meanings are shaped in literary texts	40%, 12 marks	N/A
How does Rossetti use language, form and structure to convey her ideas? What specific words, phrases and literary techniques are important in understanding her major themes and ideas?		
AO3: Demonstrate understanding of the significances and influences of the contexts in which literary texts are written and received	10%, 3 marks	50%, 15 marks
How is Rossetti affected – consciously or otherwise – by the Victorian time in which she lived? How do her religious, social and political views come across in her work? As modern readers, what do we think of her portrayal?		
AO4: Explore connections across literary texts	20%, 6 marks	25%, 7 marks
Are the themes and ideas typical of Rossetti's poems in this selection? Does she use the same concepts/interpretations? Does she use similar techniques to develop different ideas? Do you sound like you're confidently able to discuss Rossetti's poetry, rather than just a poem?		
AO5: Explore literary texts informed by different interpretations	N/A	12,5%, 3.5 marks
Can you make a balanced, detailed **argument**? Can you explore the ways that different critics, or critical viewpoints, might comment on the themes and ideas being presented in the text?		

*Although AO2 – Form, language and structure – is not **specifically** named in these objectives, it would be form a useful part of AO1-how else is the response being shaped?*

LIST OF SELECTED POEMS FOR STUDY

1. A Birthday
2. Echo
3. From the Antique
4. Goblin Market
5. Good Friday
6. In the Round Tower at Jhansi (Indian Mutiny)
7. Maude Clare
8. No Thank you, John
9. Shut Out
10. Soeur Louise de la Miséricorde
11. Song: When I am dead, my dearest
12. Remember
13. Twice
14. Up-hill
15. Winter: My Secret

My heart is like a singing bird
Whose nest is in a watered shoot;
My heart is like an apple-tree
Whose boughs are bent with thickset fruit;
My heart is like a rainbow shell
That paddles in a halcyon sea;
My heart is gladder than all these
Because my love is come to me.

Raise me a dais of silk and down;
Hang it with vair* and purple dyes;
Carve it in doves and pomegranates,
And peacocks with a hundred eyes;
Work it in gold and silver grapes,
In leaves and silver fleurs-de-lys;
Because the birthday of my life
Is come, my love is come to me

*Vair – decorative furs.

CONTEXT:

- Rossetti's religion
- Romantic poetry: William Wordsworth emphasized the importance of expressing natural feelings when he argued that it was his intention to create a poetry which was a 'spontaneous overflow of powerful feelings'

INTERPRETATION/ANALYSIS

My heart is like a singing bird
Whose nest is in a watered shoot;
My heart is like an apple-tree
Whose boughs are bent with thickset fruit;
My heart is like a rainbow shell
That paddles in a halcyon sea;
My heart is gladder than all these
Because my love is come to me.

This is an uncharacteristically happy poem! The images of nature are beautiful, full of love and promise and celebration. Unlike many of Rossetti's works which are tinged with sadness, guilt or loss, this seems to be simply pure joy.

This first stanza uses repeated similes of nature to convey the possibility and hope, the freshness of life once love is arrived. There's a slightly unusual generic nature to Rossetti's imagery here – often she names specific birds, for example, but here the use of "singing bird" implies that all of nature is "singing" and celebrating the arrival of her love. The abundance and richness of nature shows how joyful the speaker is; the "thickset fruit" and the "watered shoot" show nature at all its stages of life. The "halcyon sea" suggest peace, warmth and calm – there's almost too much pleasure to be borne. The poem is also rife with colour, with the "rainbow shell" creating a further impression of richness and lavishness. The rainbow also bears religious connotations, as a rainbow was sent by God following the flood, as a promise to Noah that such an event would never happen again. The simplicity of the final couplet of the stanza is almost heart-breaking in its joyful honesty: "Because my love is come to me."

Yet is there a note of uncertainty here, or are we searching too hard for alternate meanings? The "thickset fruit" of the apple tree might hold implications of the fall, and threaten to break the bough it lies on. The "watered shoot" is either easily disrupted and dug up, or will eventually disrupt the nest – shoots grow, and will pull it apart – and the rest of the nature here, though beautiful, is temporary and quickly ruined. Is the heart's gladness as temporary? This poem could be interpreted as being about either religious of romantic love – the "birthday of my life" in the second stanza could be the sense of renewal felt when a lover arrives, or could be a reference to a christening/confirmation and acceptance of Jesus.

Raise me a dais of silk and down;
Hang it with vair* and purple dyes;
Carve it in doves and pomegranates,
And peacocks with a hundred eyes;
Work it in gold and silver grapes,

In leaves and silver fleurs-de-lys;
Because the birthday of my life
Is come, my love is come to me

In the second stanza the richness continues, but moves inside and away from nature, to creations of mankind – the dais or platform being created to celebrate the lover is covered with rich, man-made vair and purple, a rich royal colour. The dais and its surrounding sound like a temple, created either to God or a human lover. Here, too nature is called upon and the carvings add to the celebration, symbolizing peace (doves), and fertility (pomegranate). All these symbols were in use in Victorian secular art and culture, particularly the exoticism of the pomegranate and peacock as art and design took influences form the growing British Empire. However, there is a further possibility of interpreting this poem as religious love, supported by the peacock – a symbol of all-seeing Christianity. These carvings, in wood, gold and silver, will be long-lasting, not the temporary beauty of the first stanza's natural world. Yet here, too, is it perhaps *too* beautiful, and cloying or overdone in its efforts to produce a beauty to rival nature?

Images of royalty pervade this stanza – the dais from which royalty might address a court, the royal colour of purple, the heraldic fleur-de-lys, a lily-like image often found on coats of arms. These elevate the love, or acknowledge the superior nature of God.

The poem could also be interpreted as the human impulse to create in order to memorialize love – frequently found in Rossetti's work. The natural imagery, although romanticized and beautiful, is fleeting, and so the speaker turns in the second stanza to a more permanent method of celebration and memorial.

STRUCTURE AND FORM

Lyric poem using imagery of beauty and nature, in a musical sound which focuses on exploring emotion.

Iambic tetrameter creates a song-like rhythm, consistently stressing the word "heart".

Trochees in the second verse mean stress falls on "raise", "hang", "carve" and "word", emphasizing the desire to create something new in celebration.

CRITICAL INTERPRETATION

The rich artistic details of the "dais" overshadow the impulse of love that generates its gothic artifice (note, for instance, the use of the archaic "vair"), and those details, in contrast with the natural images of the poem's first stanza, imply that the only true and permanent fulfillment of love is to be found in the art it gives birth to.

There is a further critical interpretation that *Birthday* is not religious – Lynda Palazzo, argues that Rossetti never tries to hide her religious poetry – so why would this be implied or beneath the surface? Instead, she suggests that it's an exploration of the poetic itself and Dante Gabriel Rossetti's idea that *everything* has a point at which pleasure in it becomes poetry in itself. This builds on the Romantic idea that everything should be experienced as fully as possible. So the beauty and splendor, of both the natural and the man-made worlds, are so beautiful that they are themselves poetry: pure emotion to be experienced.

CONNECTIONS:

Religion: Song; Remember; Twice
Romantic love: Maude Clare; No Thank You John; Remember; Echo
Natural imagery: Song; Maude Clare; Goblin Market; From the Antique

[1]Come to me in the silence of the night;
Come in the speaking silence of a dream;
Come with soft rounded cheeks and eyes as bright
As sunlight on a stream;
[5]Come back in tears,
O memory, hope, love of finished years.

O dream how sweet, too sweet, too bitter sweet,
Whose wakening should have been in Paradise,
Where souls brimfull of love abide and meet;
[10]Where thirsting longing eyes
Watch the slow door
That opening, letting in, lets out no more.

Yet come to me in dreams, that I may live
My very life again though cold in death:
[15]Come back to me in dreams, that I may give
Pulse for pulse, breath for breath:
Speak low, lean low
As long ago, my love, how long ago.

CONTEXT:

- Rossetti's religious beliefs, including belief in the afterlife
- Her personal life – love and family
- In the same year as this was published, Elizabeth Barrett Browning wrote *A Musical Instrument*, telling the story of the Greek god Pan who "hacked and hewed" an instrument into shape from a reed. The wider suggestion is that poetry, like the musical instrument, comes essentially from a place of suffering or deep feeling that needs expressing.
- In Greek myth, "Echo" was a nymph who helped Zeus commit adultery by distracting his wife, Hera. Once Hera found out, she made her unable to speak except to repeat someone else's last words. Echo fell in love with Narcissus but as she could only echo him, he rejected her and she pined away until only her voice remained.

> **Come to me in the silence of the night;**
> **Come in the speaking silence of a dream;**
> **Come with soft rounded cheeks and eyes as bright**
> **As sunlight on a stream;**
> **Come back in tears,**
> **O memory, hope, love of finished years.**

In many ways this is a partner poem to *Song*, from the perspective of a speaker after a loved one's death. The repeated imperative "come" sounds more like a plea every time it's repeated, rather than an instruction – this is a poem of longing, and despair. The speaker acknowledges the "silence of the night", the "silence of a dream" – the only way they will see their loved one again. Rossetti's oxymoron "speaking silence" also highlights the dreamlike quality here, where two people can communicate without words. The references to "night" and "dream" could be taken as more sexualized or passionate, but given the rest of the poem this seems less likely.

The "love of finished years", though, implies that the loved one is older – their love was ended, maybe. The triadic structure of "memory, hope, love" wraps together everything the speaker wants: to experience that relationship once again.

There's a question as to who this is about – it could read as a love returning from the grave to comfort their loved one. But the "soft rounded cheeks and eyes as bright/as sunlight on a stream" suggests someone younger, perhaps – a sister or child, maybe.

Especially given the meaning of "Echo" – the repeated sound – it's unsurprising that sound plays an incredibly important part in this poem; this begins in the first stanza with the repetition of "come" and the sibilance of "silence...speaking silence...sunlight on a stream", a soft, gentle repeated sound.

> **O dream how sweet, too sweet, too bitter sweet,**
> **Whose wakening should have been in Paradise,**
> **Where souls brimfull of love abide and meet;**
> **Where thirsting longing eyes**
> **Watch the slow door**
> **That opening, letting in, lets out no more.**

The exclamative "o dream" is filled with longing and regret; repetition of "sweet" with its changes until it becomes "bittersweet" as the speaker realizes they are not waking in "Paradise", but instead are merely in a dream, not seeing their loved one again after all.

Here, too, is a suggestion of passion – the souls "abide and meet" with "thirsting longing eyes", the active verbs highlighting the speaker's desperation to see this person again. That their "souls" meet again reminds us of the dreamlike quality of this encounter, but also the religious possibilities -a soul sent from heaven to comfort, perhaps. Here the dominant sounds are soft "w"s and "l"s, a gentle soft sound, pleading almost, or breathless.

The short line "watch the slow door" creates a sense of hesitation and anticipation before it opens. The door is a frequent image in Rossetti's poetry; here it is "slow", and watched – "that opening, letting in, lets out no more" – the door to heaven opens only one way and cannot let the loved one out.

> **Yet come to me in dreams, that I may live**
> **My very life again though cold in death:**
> **Come back to me in dreams, that I may give**
> **Pulse for pulse, breath for breath:**
> **Speak low, lean low**
> **As long ago, my love, how long ago.**

Echoing the beginning "Come in the speaking silence of a dream", Rossetti uses the oxymoron of living life after death, drawing on religious understandings of the afterlife to find comfort. Again, though, this might also sound a more passionate dream, particularly with the "pulse for pulse, breath for breath", lovers matching one another's very physical actions, the physicality needed for life.

STRUCTURE AND FORM

- **Lyric** – the lyric was originally Ancient Greek, using intensely musical language and rhythm, focusing on emotion rather than narrative – conveying feeling above all else. Originally they were written to be sung, accompanied by a lyre, but in the Victorian era it became a more printed form.
- **Repetition** – using the concept of the "echo", Rossetti uses a variety of repetition techniques to emphasize her language, including: **Anaphora** (repeating at the beginning of the phrase) –"come"; **Alliteration** (words beginning with the same sound) – "letting in lets out", "whose/where/watch"; **Sibilance** "speaking silence, sunlight on a stream"; **Parallelisms** (repeated phrasing structures): "Pulse for pulse, breath for breath"
- **Rhyme scheme** – each stanza has an ababcc rhyme scheme, suggesting the movement of the speaker's feelings. It's relatively fragmented; the rhymes don't continue through the stanzas. Some rhymes emphasize their opposites – "night/bright", "death/breath" to signify the essential conflict here of life and

death. "Paradise/eyes" in the second stanza is more of a half-rhyme signalling a moment of doubt when the speaker realises fully that the dream is not enough.

- **Trochees** are used in the first three lines ("come to, come in, come with," to convey urgency and passion.
- **Metre** – the "**Pulse** for **pulse**, **breath** for **breath**" is suddenly interrupted trochees, and highlights the physicality of the language, as well as the breathlessness of the speaker In this moment.
- **Motif** of water is used – the stream, tears, thirsting – but it's n unusually mournful image (water is often used to signify life) so perhaps Rossetti is drawing on more Greek imagery of the River Styx or Lethe – two of the rivers used to cross into the after-world, and after crossing Lethe, all memory is dissipated.

CONNECTIONS

The afterlife: Twice; Remember: Song; Shut Out
Love: Remember; No Thank You John;
Longing: Remember; Song; Shut Out; From the Antique
Silence: Winter: My Secret; Shut Out; Goblin Market; Echo; Remember

14

[1]It's a weary life, it is, she said:
Doubly blank is a woman's lot:
I wish and I wish I were a man:
Or, better then any being, were not:

[5]Were nothing at all in all the world,
Not a body and not a soul:
Not so much as a grain of dust
Or a drop of water from pole to pole.

Still the world would wag on the same,
[10]Still the seasons go and come:
Blossoms bloom as in days of old,
Cherries ripen and wild bees hum.

None would miss me in all the world,
How much less would care or weep:
[15]I should be nothing, while all the rest
Would wake and weary and fall asleep.

CONTEXT:

This was composed in Rossetti's in 1854 but never published in Rossetti's lifetime possibly because of its unmistakable critique – the poem opens with an unflinching expression of despair. "Wearying" is a woman's position that the lack of existence is preferable, because of the need to escape gender expectations.

The poem implies a concern with the duality a woman faces- the inability to see herself as important yet, to ourselves, aren't we always?

-   Attitude towards women's rights and independence

INTERPRETATION / ANALYSIS

It's a weary life, it is, she said:
Doubly blank in a woman's lot:
I wish and I wish I were a man:
Or, better then any being, were not:

Rossetti begins this lyric poem from the perspective of a speaker – the "she" suggests not Rossetti herself but a speaker. The "weariness" is echoed in much Victorian poetry (Tennyson's *Mariana*'s refrain "I am aweary") highlighting the emptiness and dreary nature of a life that is so restricted. Simon Avery calls the word choice "austere", noting its cold, bleak nature.

Is Rossetti talking about all women, or a particular **class** of women here? Rossetti herself was relatively comfortable – although the family suffered financial difficulties they were never considered to be working class. Rossetti was also very involved with working class women through her work with 'unfortunates' and single mothers; she's often concerned for the plight of all women. Working class women often actually have more freedom in some respects because their financial circumstances dictate they go into the world and work – is this "weariness" actually a little self-indulgent from a middle-class woman given the hardships working women often experience?

Does this single speaker speak for herself, or is "she" in fact all women? The metrical changes at the beginning of the stanza emphasize the phrase "doubly blank" to highlight the emptiness of the female world.

By writing "she said", Rossetti also distances herself from her speaker, allowing her the ability to speak/write more freely while hiding behind the pretence of being a character. The duality – "doubly"- holds views that she may wish to express, and allowing herself as a writer the ability to refute her own writing: perhaps a reason why *From the Antique* was not published within her lifetime.

Note her religious views on feminist issues though (be aware the term "feminist" is anachronistic – nobody at the time would have used the word) as Rossetti believed women should be <u>well treated and respected</u> but not equal politically – she was opposed to women's university education, and signed petitions against female suffrage, for example. Her beliefs stem from the biblical understanding that woman comes from, and is therefore subject to, man: to give her the vote would create a false equality. Women should be prized for their feminine qualities – compassion, morality, support and guidance etc – but are not the same as men and the sexes should be treated differently.

The repetition of "I wish" highlights the futility of her desire – the syndetic structure[1] ("and") also has the effect of adding a fairy-tale quality to the line- also highlighting its lack of reality. She would prefer being nothing (note though – not **dead** merely **nothing**) than being a woman.

---

[1] Of or using conjunctions.

Were nothing at all in all the world,
Not a body and not a soul:
Not so much as a grain of dust
Or a drop of water from pole to pole.

The subjunctive "Were" is used to highlight the importance of the statement, and the sense of possibility (although this is misleading – there **is no** possibility here) Rossetti separates the body and soul – prefacing both with the "not" to indicate that there is no separation, perhaps, of the two – the body and soul are both female and therefore neither should exist. The line "not so much as a grain of dust" holds echoes of the funeral service – "ashes to ashes, dust to dust", calling on religious ideas of the body's impermanence in contrast to that of the soul. Lacking "dust" and "water", the earth surely ceases to be – and so, Rossetti's speaker argues that were her body and soul reduced to dust and water, there would still be no mourning or even notice of their disappearance.

The whole second stanza is this conditional imaginary scenario – if I cease to be, reminiscent of Keats' *"When I have fears that I may cease to be"* (1818, see end) in which the poet imagines a fear of not leaving his mark on the world, but makes peace with the "wide world" he experiences. While Keats is comforted ultimately by his lack of importance in the world – standing on the edge of it, "alone", Rossetti's speaker is not so peaceful.

Still the world would wag on the same,
Still the seasons go and come:
Blossoms bloom as in days of old,
Cherries ripen and wild bees hum.

The conditional "were" of the second stanza is answered in this stanza's opening with a more definitive "would": "still the world would wag on the same." "Wag" almost seems dismissive, reminding of wagging tongues, gossip of little consequence. Is this anger and bitterness, causing her to reject the world itself as meaningless (perhaps in some ways more like Keats and his comfort that "love and fame to nothingness do sink"?) or is it an attempt to comfort herself by insisting that the lack of consequence in the world is not limited to her alone? Her obliteration from the world would count for nothing, and nobody would notice or care – but the world would keep on turning if she is not there and is that perhaps an indication that Rossetti isn't as sympathetic as might first be thought?

The speaker turns to nature – as Keats so often does – and identifies the "blossoms", "cherries" and "bees" – all short-lived, temporary and quick to fade away yet they are more permanent through their repeated life-cycles than she will be. It's interesting that

17

in this poem there's little religious comfort to be had other than the eternal nature of the earth. The seasons "go and come"; the inversion of the usual collocation[2] has an almost dream-like quality in the rhythm here, as well as enabling Rossetti to complete the "come/hum" rhyme scheme.

> **None would miss me in all the world,**
> **How much less would care or weep:**
> **I should be nothing, while all the rest**
> **Would wake and weary and fall asleep.**

The blunt short line "None would miss me in all the world." brooks no argument, end-stopped to heighten her sense of defiance – or despair?

Rossetti changes the tense from the subjunctive "were" to the modal "should" – a change indicating that there is a decision being made at the end; the "should" is far more final.

The final line's actions "wake and weary and fall asleep" has an unsettled rhythm; the "weary" seeming out of place. The change of "weary" from adjective in line 1 ("it's a weary life") to verb in the final line "would wake and weary" *may* suggest a change in perspective. A woman's life is weary – dreary, boring and dull – but the people in the world "weary" – do they *become* weary, or weary others? Yet it seems likely that she's suggesting that, like the speaker herself, others in the world will also find their lives weary. Is this an indication that she's speaking of women in general – or is it even broader than that? Does she count the rest of humanity as equally worthless, in some regards, and so an individual's feeling weary or unimportant is in fact itself actually quite selfish and they should realize their place in the wider world?

The final "asleep" brings back the previous suggestion of nothingness – the passing of conscious into unconsciousness, the "not" that afflicts the entire second stanza.

---

[2] A collocation is a sequence of words or terms that co-occur more often than would be expected by chance.

18

STRUCTURE AND FORM

- **Metrically unstable** – alternates between 8, 9 and 10 syllables and between iambs and anapests. This creates a more naturalistic rhythm but also sometimes catches off-guard – the final line seems to be cut short, for example.
- **Regular ABCB rhyme scheme:** To an extent off-sets the unstable meter; the abcb rhyme scheme leaves each stanza feeling complete, while the regular pacing of the stanzas – four quatrains – also implies a regularity which could reflect the dullness of the speaker's existence.

CRITICAL INTERPRETATIONS

"As Simone de Beauvoir has pointed out, in a patriarchal culture woman inevitably experiences herself as object and other. The problem is especially acute during adolescence when woman must make herself into or pretend to be an alluring object. Then "the very face itself becomes a mask"".

Dolores Rosenblum, *Christina Rossetti: the inward pose* in 'Shakespeare's sisters: feminist essays on women poets' ed. Sandra Gilbert and Susan Gubar

> When I have fears that I may cease to be
>   Before my pen has gleaned my teeming brain,
> Before high-pilèd books, in charactery,
>   Hold like rich garners the full ripened grain;
> When I behold, upon the night's starred face,
>   Huge cloudy symbols of a high romance,
> And think that I may never live to trace
>   Their shadows with the magic hand of chance;
> And when I feel, fair creature of an hour,
>   That I shall never look upon thee more,
> Never have relish in the faery power
>   Of unreflecting love—then on the shore
> Of the wide world I stand alone, and think
> Till love and fame to nothingness do sink.
>
> John Keats

CONNECTIONS

<u>Women's difficulties in society</u> – No, Thank You John; Winter: My Secret; Shut Out; Soeur Louise
<u>Imagery of nature:</u> Shut Out; Goblin Market; A Birthday
<u>Melancholy tone:</u> Song (When I am dead); Remember

19

Because *Goblin Market* is such a long and complex poem – entire books have been written about it! – I'm approaching this one slightly differently. The full text is at the end of the guide. Below, you'll find a quick summary of the key interpretations, and some idea of the technical basis for this interpretation, though there'll be plenty more in the whole poem. You wouldn't be expected to know the whole poem, and if it's named on the paper only a section will be used, of course – but it's worth really getting to grips with this one, because it can link to virtually everything in the rest of the collection.

While *Goblin Market* can be read as a children's fairytale -and Rossetti insisted in public that's what it was – there's also far darker interpretations, and privately in a letter to her publisher, Christina said it shouldn't be marketed to children – an interesting conflict to bear in mind!

INTERPRETATION: CHILDREN'S FAIRYTALE

Morality tales for children were very common, often quite twee or clichéd, with a very obvious moral towards the end. Louis Carrol, in *Alice in Wonderland*, mocked these when Alice has a conversation with the Duchess about finding morals in other tales. *Goblin Market* can be read as a fable for children in which Laura's curiosity nearly causes her death (and does in fact cause Jeannie's), but in the end she's saved by her sister's love and the two of them go on to have happy, loving lives. Moral? Curiosity is bad, don't look outside your world – but you can be rescued by a loving family.

Evidence

*   The goblin creatures, common in fairytales, and described in animalistic terms but at least to begin with not frightening – more like woodland animals.
*   Relative simplicity of vocabulary and syntax
*   The balladesque narrative, which creates a story-like quality, like a fairytale
*   The happy ending when balance is restored - Laura and Lizzie are "wives/with children of their own" and warn their own children

INTERPRETATION: SEX AND SEXUALITY

"Curious Laura" explores her sexuality with the Goblin men, who are at first animalistic but become more masculine as the poem continues. She experiences it with pure desire and lust, but her preoccupation with returning for more threatens to destroy her (link: *Soeur Louise*). Jeannie is the cautionary tale of a girl who similarly experienced desire, and it brought her death (perhaps a comment on the dangers of pregnancy and death in childbirth?) Lizzie, who remains stoic and refuses to give into desire, saves her sister. Even though Lizzie *experiences* the fruit of the goblins, she doesn't *enjoy* it, and therefore is in some ways the ideal virtuous Victorian woman (*Link: Maude Clare, From the Antique*)

The poem explores rape and masculine power, in the goblins' assault on Lizzie as they "push their fruits against her mouth", for example; the men are wholly in control in this poem. There's also a glimmer of homosexuality (and therefore incest), when Lizzie encourages Laura to "hug me, kiss me, suck my juices".

Yet as ever with Rossetti there's a conflicting undertone – by the end, there's no real difference between Laura and Lizzie. They both marry happily and have children (the pinnacle of feminine success?!) and so is this a protest that 'fallen women' shouldn't be made to suffer for the rest of their lives, as Jeannie is? (*Link: Winter: My Secret*)

Evidence

- Contrasting descriptions of Laura and Lizzie in their encounters with the goblins. Similarities with Jeannie. Look in particular a the colours and animal imagery of the girls (white, swan etc.) and the way they move – veiled versus looking
- Description of the rape of Lizzie
- Happy ending resolution
- Contrast of the two sisters' actions

INTERPRETATION: PRESENTATION OF MASCULINTIY

Probably the most negative of Rossetti's portrayals of men! The goblin creatures are animalistic, vicious and controlling – they exert complete power over the girls they tempt. And they **do** tempt; it's their calls that bring Laura in, then when they have what they wanted from her they cast her aside, not caring that she is ruined (*Link: From the Antique, Winter: My Secret*). Rossetti's work at the women's refuge made her angry about the double standards for men and women – for women to be prostitutes, men must be buying their services! They assault Lizzie viciously and sexually, and they take both a part of Laura (her hair) and money from Lizzie, indicating that they take everything from a woman, perhaps a critique of the marriage laws restricting property ownership.

Evidence

- Animalistic descriptions of the goblins
- Goblins' vicious, active verbs as they assault Lizzie
- Disappearance of men at the end – although the girls are wives and mothers, their husbands aren't mentioned.

INTERPRETATION: CRITIQUE OF COMMERCE IN THE VICTORIAN ERA

The Goblins' market cries sell fruit, a rarity and expensive in the era although becoming increasingly common with the improvements in trade, refrigeration and so on. There's an abundance of it, maybe even too much, suggesting a critique of the consumerism that started with the Victorian development of the leisured classes, increasing wealth n the middle class, and ways to display that wealth. Cities also emerged in the era, and brought with them a moral panic and concern because of the close proximity of a huge population, influx of prostitutes, criminals and others considered to be an 'underclass', along with the movement of young people away from the family home completely changing the landscape of family relationships. Herbert Tucker has suggested that the techniques of the Goblins when trying to persuade Lizzie to buy from them are similar to complaints made about the rise of advertising in the era.

There's also an argument which looks at the poem as a critique of the marriage market in the era – what women can bring to a marriage determining their value (*Link: Maude Clare, No Thank You John*)

Evidence

- Abundance of the fruit which is "all ripe together" no matter what the season, as farmers/grocers started trying to manipulate growing times to suit a demanding population
- Laura's temptation to buy and buy
- The exchanges – Laura's gold hair, and Lizzie's coin
- Listing of the fruits – chaotic, noisy and aggressive
- Repeated language of sweetness in the goblins' allure – *maybe* a reference to the growth of sugar by slaves in America as the civil war was continuing (although this is

speculative) . Juxtapose this slightly underhanded production with Lizzie and Laura's wholesome domestic productivity

INTERPRETATION: RELIGIOUS NARRATIVE OF SALVATION AND SACRIFICE

Laura is humanity, an allegory for Eve's sin committed by seeking out the fruit from the goblins as Eve sought the fruit from the tree of knowledge. When she obtains it, she is lost – her sinfulness is shown in her lack of interest in life and loss of industry, drawing on the Puritan/Christian work ethic, believing that hard work is a way to praise God.

Lizzie's self-sacrifice mirrors that of Christ. As he was crucified on the cross, Lizzie is assaulted by the Goblin men. She returns to Laura, and her words echo the Eucharist, the sacrament following the Last Supper when Jesus said to his disciples drink this wine and eat this bread, for it is my blood and flesh – the ritual on which Communion is founded. Lizzie's feeding of Laura is a close allegory of this ritual. (*Link: Song, Remember, Good Friday, Birthday*)

Evidence

- The listing of fruit (acknowledging too that the fruit in the Bible isn't specific as an apple)
- Laura's return – "suck my juices"
- Self-sacrificing language describing Laura during the Goblin attack
- Redemptive ending: both sisters are saved

INTERPRETATION: WOMANHOOD AND POWER

Sandra Gilbert has suggested that the fruit is access to the artistic world – being sold by men and for women to enter they have to give up so much of themselves, the worth is questionable. Laura wants to be a part of it but it destroys her femininity – her ability to complete the domestic and moral tasks she is responsible for. Laura is creative and free, but that destroys her, and she must learn to control it to be a responsible mother. (*Link: Birthday*)

The girls are portrayed as the two sides of women – vice and virtue – although Laura is forgiven her misdemeanours. A "happy ending" is the two girls as wives and mothers, telling their own children morality tales. It's perhaps a bit of a disappointing ending in some respects as after such a dark luscious tale, the girls return to a very stereotypical femininity. Yet Rossetti is a Victorian after all! (*Link: Winter: My Secret, Maude Clare, From the Antique*)

Evidence

23

- Description of the two girls as "maids", virginal colours, sweet and elegant creatures
- The language of desire including enjambment when Laura's intense need is being described speeding the pace
- Ending with them both as wives and mothers

INTERPRETATION: AN ADDICTION NARRATIVE

The way Laura reacts to the goblins is classic addition – she grows pale, thin, listless and loses interest in anything else. All she can focus on is finding the next 'fix', the next opportunity to see the goblins and get some more fruit. Jeannie, who went before her, is dead of a similar addiction, perhaps through overdose. While this poem pre-dates the addictions of Dante Gabriel and Lizzie Siddal, there are striking similarities in the descriptions of Laura's state post-goblin to an addict's withdrawal symptoms.

Evidence

- Description of Laura as pale, thin, losing interest in the world around her
- The "juices" functioning as a sort of methadone– a substitute used to wean addicts off the drug
- References to Jeannie's destruction, first through what's thinly veiled prostitution and then through death perhaps by overdone.

INTERPRETATION: ELEMENTS OF THE GOTHIC

The Goblin men are a typical monstrous feature of Gothic literature – used as ciphers through which to explore the monstrous nature of mankind. Whether Rochester's supernatural voice in *Jane Eyre* or the vampiric *Dracula*, the powers and desires of men are frequently exhibited through other-worldly creatures.

The two sisters could also be considered **doubles** – two sides of one person, a common Gothic feature (consider Jane Eyre and Bertha Mason, for example). Laura is the darker, curious side, while Lizzie is the good urges of women.

- They often *act* similarly but are *described* differently e.g. looking / veiled her eyes
- All the darker urges are in one, the selfless nature in the other

GOBLIN MARKET: STRUCTURE AND FORM

Meter:

Mostly written in iambic tetrameter creating the rhythmic, fast pace – the passion of the story, as well as the iambic rhythm echoing natural speech, as though this is a fairytale read aloud in the oral tradition. However, there are many variations, interruptions and changes throughout the poem for different purposes.

Most of the language associated with goblins is dactylic dimeter – a sense of incantation and, particularly with the listing of the fruits, speeds the pace further to add to the sense of abundance and loss of control.

Lizzie shouts "no, no, no" – interrupting the rhythm, as well as exclaiming to stop Laura

Laura's physical illness: "fetched honey', 'brought water', 'sat down') verbally indicate the way in which Laura is physically 'seizing up' as her illness takes hold

In the description of Laura's recovery, spondees are used to give emphasis to the power of the antidote that Lizzie brings her. The repetition of the same initial letters in the phrases 'Swift fire' and 'Sense failed' (lines 507-513) further increases the sense of the rush of life that overcomes Laura as she recovers.

Rhyme

The irregular yet insistent rhyme carries the poem forwards. The poem contains numerous couplets which occur especially in its lists. This increases the speed at which the poem is read and creates a rushed and breathless feel. For instance, by framing the goblin's cry using couplets and triplets, Rossetti emphasizes its speed and draws attention to its overwhelming nature as it overpowers listeners with variety and quantity of description.

Repeated imagery

Roots and shoots, including the fruit – searching for knowledge, the idea that the fruit/knowledge reduces growth and fertility, and happiness.

Fruit – symbolic of knowledge and curiosity, references to the biblical fruit as well as temptation more generally

Hair – a huge cultural commodity and very popular in the Pre-Raphaelite brotherhood as a metaphor. Hair was put into bracelets and necklaces as keepsakes and memorials. Throughout the poetry of the period, women's hair has been variously depicted as a weapon, a veil, a snare, a web and a noose. Laura's exchange of hair for fruit is also metaphoric of prostitution, handing over herself to the men.

Narrative structure

The poem tells the story from a third person perspective, so sounds more like an orally-transmitted fairytale than a written piece. It's designed to be read aloud in that tradition. The atory begins close to the centre of the action with the two girls seeing the market appear. The height of tension is Lizzie's travelling to the market and her exchange/assault. The story is resolved when both girls are happy wives and mothers, apparently fulfilled.

FURTHER READING:

The Possibilities of Interpretation in Christina Rossetti's "Goblin Market" (Gaynell Galt)
https://www.lagrange.edu/resources/pdf/citations/2009/13English_Galt.pdf

Sugar-Baited Words: The Erotic Commerce of *Goblin Market* (Juliet O'Keefe)-
http://www3.telus.net/sargassosea/gm.html

Christina Rossetti's *Goblin Market* Finding the Middle Ground (Jasmine Yeh)
https://depts.washington.edu/egonline/2010/04/2008-09-winner-christina-rossetti%e2%80%99s-goblin-market-finding-the-middle-ground-by-jasmine-yeh/#more-41

The Woman Question; Sisterhood, sexuality and subversion in Rossetti's *Goblin Market* (Author unknown) https://olympe.files.wordpress.com/2007/06/essay-goblins-rossetti.pdf

It's also worth looking at this site for some of the artwork that's accompanied *Goblin Market* over the years – ranging from the originals by Dante Gabriel, through Arthur Hughes' fairylike illustrations (he also illustrated *Alice* and *Peter Pan*) and the Playboy illustrations, which leaves little to th imagination!
https://britlitsurvey2.wordpress.com/2014/04/30/the-sensual-and-the-vulgar-100-years-of-illustrated-goblin-market/

¹Am I a stone, and not a sheep,
That I can stand, O Christ, beneath Thy cross,
To number drop by drop Thy blood's slow loss,
And yet not weep?

⁵Not so those women loved
Who with exceeding grief lamented Thee;
Not so fallen Peter weeping bitterly;
Not so the thief was moved;

Not so the Sun and Moon
¹⁰Which hid their faces in a starless sky,
A horror of great darkness at broad noon—
I, only I.

Yet give not o'er,
But seek Thy sheep, true Shepherd of the flock;
¹⁵Greater than Moses, turn and look once more
And smite a rock.

CONTEXT

- Rossetti's ideas about religion
- Rossetti's attitudes towards women

Good Friday is a Holy Day commemorating the crucifixion of Jesus Christ at Calvary. The Easter celebration is the most important in the Christian calendar, as it's the point at which Jesus died to redeem Mankind.

INTERPRETATION / ANALYSIS

Am I a stone, and not a sheep,
That I can stand, O Christ, beneath Thy cross,
To number drop by drop Thy blood's slow loss,
And yet not weep?

The questioning tone of this poem reveals its major concerns: Religious doubt. The speaker is deeply conflicted about their ability to belief wholly and whole-heartedly, and to feel the emotions that they think are *appropriate* to worship – they want to be able to love and mourn Jesus with their whole heart. However, there are also questions raised about why they think those emotions are appropriate, and whether their faith is enough as it is. Unusually for this selection (although it appears elsewhere in Rossetti's poetry), the speaker addresses Christ directly, an exclamative separated by caesura from the rest of the line, which gives the poem the air of a prayer. The sibilance of "Stone", "sheep" and "stand" create a sense of tiredness, that these questions have all been asked before and the speaker is despairing of receiving a satisfactory response.

Several images recur through the poem – the sheep and stone in particular, which have religious symbolism. The stone is reference in the Book of Exodus – Moses, when taking his people out of Egypt to seek their own land, is instructed by God: "Strike the rock and water will come out of it for the people to drink." When Moses does, water comes forth and he saves his people through his faith. So the reference here, which is repeated with a closer Biblical allusion in the final stanza, is a commentary on doubt – the speaker at the beginning uses the stone as a symbol of an immovable object which cannot feel or think or respond to God. The sheep, however, uses the common metaphor fo the "flock" of the congregation, and Christ is often referred to as a shepherd, guiding them. Yet the image of the dumb sheep who simply follows is also brought to mind – Rossetti's speaker cannot even muster as much emotion as this.

The speaker laments their coldness – they "number drop by drop" the blood loss, observing in minute detail every moment of Christ's death, yet can't weep.

> **Not so those women loved**
> **Who with exceeding grief lamented Thee;**
> **Not so fallen Peter weeping bitterly;**
> **Not so the thief was moved;**

Rossetti begins with a trochee ("Not so") which interrupts the previously iambic rhythm and shows the difficulty the speaker's experiencing. The repetitive negative creates a crowd of people who do not respond the same way – neither the women, Peter, nor the thief who is also there. These refer to different people present at Christ's death. Accounts differ, but most mention Jesus' mother Mary, and Mary Magdalene, sometimes with a following of other women. Peter was one of Jesus' disciples who, when questioned, denied Christ three times, a betrayal Christ had predicted (hence the "fallen"). There are two thieves, one on either side – one who asks Christ to remember him (likely the one in this poem, as he's the penitent one more likely to be grieving), and one who asks why Christ can't save himself. These references include a broad spectrum of people all of whom are able to mourn for Christ, juxtaposed with the speaker's lack of crying. The "exceeding grief" is an interesting phrase; while it's appropriate for women to grieve for Christ, Victorian values had very strict understandings on what an appropriate level of grief was, even setting rules for length and style of mourning. Their emotions are emphasized by the enjambment of the stanza placing "loved", "lamented Thee", "bitterly" and "moved" on the ends of the lines.

28

Not so the Sun and Moon
Which hid their faces in a starless sky,
A horror of great darkness at broad noon—
I, only I.

The Sun and Moon are personified here as they "hid their faces" – even great heavenly bodies are so affected by the death that they must look away. This is a further Biblical reference as Luke's gospel refers to the darkness spreading over the earth and the sun being hidden for a time as though in mourning. The "starless sky" and "great darkness at broad noon" imply a deeply unnatural and dangerous darkness which is horrifying. Yet still the speaker does not week or look away. Here, there's a slightly different view emerging – the "I, only I", with its changed rhythm and caesura, emphasizes that only the speaker is able to look on the crucifixion – but surely, looking on it is also important – somebody must be able to bear witness, and while the others are weeping and hiding their faces, the speaker – perhaps bravely after all – looks on.

Yet give not o'er,
But seek Thy sheep, true Shepherd of the flock;
Greater than Moses, turn and look once more
And smite a rock.

The final stanza begins with a plea to Jesus not to give up on the speaker, and the poem picks up its prayer-like tone again. The speaker begs Jesus to "seek" them, to bring them back into the flock as a lost sheep would be sought after. When she names Jesus as "Greater than Moses", Rossetti reaffirms the Christian belief that although Moses was a great leader and Prophet, Jesus was the Son of God and therefore by his death can redeem Mankind. The caesura addressing Jesus – "true Shepherd of the flock" – lends a sense of weight to her plea. On the second to last line, the caesura before "turn and look once more" pauses the reader momentarily to capture the moment when the speaker is once again able to feel more emotion. The final line "and smite a rock", with its consonant ending and short deliberate tone ends on a relatively hopeful note in comparison, that they will be able to experience the level of faith and feeling that they wish.

STRUCTURE AND FORM

Short lines to end each stanza; each emphasizes the difficulty the speaker is experiencing and their lack of understanding of their own response

Rhyming couplets in the middle of the first two stanzas suggest the trapped feeling of the speaker as they're trying to break out and fully experience their emotions. The change in stanza three, removing the rhyme but retaining the iambic pentameter, suggests that the speaker is beginning to experience, and come to terms with the way that *they* experience God

Iambic rhythm for the most part emphasizes key words – "I", "stone", grief", "loss" and so on.

Interruption of "I, only I is a changed rhythm, and emphasizes the fact that the speaker's the only one who can look on what is happening.

CRITICAL INTERPRETATIONS

"Good Friday is a passionate outcry against the easy indifference with which man can think of the Christ who bore our shame in agony".

Myra Reynolds, 1898

CONNECTIONS

<u>Religion</u> – Twice; Up-hill; Shut out
<u>Doubt</u> – Twice, Remember
<u>Natural Imagery</u> – Goblin Market; Shut Out; Maude Clare

June 8., 1857 (Indian Mutiny)

A hundred, a thousand to one: even so;
Not a hope in the world remained:
The swarming howling wretches below
 Gained and gained and gained.

Skene looked at his pale young wife.   *5*
Is the time come?'—'The time is come.'
Young, strong, and so full of life,
The agony struck them dumb.

Close his arm about her now,
Close her cheek to his,   *10*
Close the pistol to her brow—
God forgive them this!

'Will it hurt much?' 'No, mine own:
I wish I could bear the pang for both.'—
'I wish I could bear the pang alone: *15*
Courage, dear, I am not loth.'

Kiss and kiss: 'It is not pain
Thus to kiss and die.
One kiss more.'—'And yet one again.'—
'Good-bye.'—'Good-bye.'   *20*

CONTEXT:

-   Roles of masculinity and femininity
-   Empire / nationhood

This poem was written in response to a newspaper article reporting that, under attack by rebels, Captain Skene ordered his wife and all other Christians in Jhansi to retreat to a tower where they attempted to defend themselves. Unable to do so, Captain Skene killed his wife and then himself to prevent them being taken prisoner. However, this account was later found to be inaccurate, - Skene and his wife were taken prisoner and executed by the mutineers.

The Indian Rebellion of 1857 was an Indian rebellion, which continued for about a year, against the rule of the British East India Company. The rebellion's also known as India's first war of independence, and contributed to the dissolution of the East India Company, with the British reorganizing the government and administration to take direct control as the British Raj. Rossetti added a footnote in an 1875 publication, after the revised accounts of the incident were revealed: 'I retain this little poem, not as historically accurate, but as written and published before I heard the supposed facts of its first verse contradicted

INTERPRETATION / ANALYSIS

> **A hundred, a thousand to one: even so;**
> **Not a hope in the world remained:**
> **The swarming howling wretches below**
> **Gained and gained and gained.**

We begin in the middle of the violent, swirling storm – *in media res*, in the midst of the action. The hyperbolic "hundred, a thousand to one" sets this up as being a narrative poem of heroism and daring, the victimized in the tower fighting against the odds without a "hope in the world". The active gerunds "swarming howling" are animalistic, portraying the rebelling "wretches" as vicious, uncaring, and aggressive. The syndetic "gained and gained and gained", along with the rhythmic pace, in the final line creates a sense of forward movement, unstoppable as they advance on the tower.

> **Skene looked at his pale young wife.**
> **Is the time come?'—'The time is come.'**
> **Young, strong, and so full of life,**
> **The agony struck them dumb.**

The reference to simply "Skene", ignoring his title, implies that Rossetti expects her reader to know the story, and to bring their own inferences to her poem. The portrayal of his wife is very stereotypical of Victorian femininity; she's unnamed, simply referred to as "his" wife, defined entirely by her relationship with Skene. She is "pale" and "young", a highlighting her defenselessness and her vulnerability, relying on Skene for protection. The sparing use of dialogue, repeating ";Is the time come?' 'The time is come'" is short, clipped and implies the strength and nobility of the British under fire (see *Critical Interpretations* for a further post-colonial interpretation of this poem). The tragedy is further exacerbated by her emotive language - "Young, strong and so full of life" – designed to make the reader empathize with the two brave young people, trapped in this terrible situation.

> **Close his arm about her now,**
> **Close her cheek to his,**
> **Close the pistol to her brow—**
> **God forgive them this!**

32

Repetition of "close" emphasizes their relationship and reliance on one another, seeking comfort in their marriage. Here they are slightly more equal as we begin with "his arm" and then it's "her cheek", but Skene remains the dominant figure, embracing his wife to physically protect her with his body. His 'noble protection' also extends to shooting her, and then himself – taking on the burden of her death so she need not do it herself. The interrupting exclamative "God forgive them" reminds us that suicide is a sin, but argues that there is no nobler option in this case, than to prevent themselves being taken by the rebels.

> 'Will it hurt much?' 'No, mine own:
> I wish I could bear the pang for both.'—
> 'I wish I could bear the pang alone:
> Courage, dear, I am not loth.'

Here, too, Skene remains the stoic protector comforting his frightened wife. The dialogue remains sparse, but gives an impression of the closeness of their relationship. Referring to their deaths as a "pang" diminishes the pain, but also demonstrates the bravery of the couple, refusing to view death as something more dangerous and frightening than the revels outside. The back-and-forth here is also slightly clichéd in its reassurance to one another, perhaps lacking a sense of genuine love – but perfectly suited to the portrayal of two brave young people sacrificing themselves.

The lack of attribution in the dialogue makes it sound more immediate, and creates a sense of intimacy in this desperate moment, but there is no danger of not being able to distinguish one from the other; the wife's speech seeks reassurance and Skene's delivers it.

> Kiss and kiss: 'It is not pain
> Thus to kiss and die.
> One kiss more.'—'And yet one again.'—
> 'Good-bye.'—'Good-bye.'

Repetition of "kiss" through this stanza emphasizes again the intimacy of the relationship, and the self-sacrificing nature of the couple. The "goodbye" at the end provides the sense of finality, without specifically writing any details of the death which would not have been appropriate for Rossetti's publication.

STRUCTURE AND FORM

Ballad form Some elements of the ballad, including the regular ABAB rhyme scheme in each quatrain, creating a quick pace suited to the active content, and the tragic narrative being told.

Enjambment in each stanza also contributes to the quickening pace, mirroring the fast nature of the decisions being made.

CRITICAL INTERPRETATION

There's a post-colonial interpretation of much Victorian literature of this type which views a large swathe of the British population as what we would now term racist (although the term is anachronistic, wouldn't have been used then). People from other lands, specifically those controlled as part of the British Empire, are often represented as savages, uncivilized with monstrous characteristics. They are often "other", a literary term fairly simply meaning anyone contrasting with the dominant narrative – which is white Victorian British. Think about Bertha in *Jane Eyre*, the mad Creole in the attic who's described as vampiric, animalistic. In Kipling's poetry, he stresses the "white man's burden", the moral imperative to rescue the "other" from their own savage destruction. While this is not the place for an in-depth discussion on the pros and cons of the British

A lithograph (1857) of the Skenes sheltering in the Tower

Empire, it is worth acknowledging that for the majority of British Victorian citizens, who never went anywhere but their own country, many genuinely thought they had a Christian duty to bring British values to less enlightened citizens of the world.

The animalistic impressions of the Indians in Rossetti's poetry seems to be worth viewing through this post-colonial lens, as the mass of people at the bottom tower is a homogenous swarm (that word itself has startlingly modern connotations in terms of racist views of other peoples – consider the use of it in the Rwandan genocide, for example, and the current debate about such language in relationship to Syrian refugees in Europe). Her choice to focus on the couple in the tower also juxtaposes the Captain's nobility and moral strength, dying to defend his wife and sacrificing himself rather than be beaten, with the savagery and total immorality expressed in the first stanza, fulfilling the British Empire's view of itself as moral, above all else.

CONNECTIONS

<u>Relationships</u> – No, Thank You, John; Goblin Market; Maude Clare
<u>Presentation of women</u> – Maude Clare; Soeur Louise; From the Antique; Good Friday
<u>Sacrifice</u> – Remember; Song; Good Friday

Out of the church she followed them
With a lofty step and mien:
His bride was like a village maid,
Maude Clare was like a queen.

"Son Thomas, " his lady mother said,
With smiles, almost with tears:
"May Nell and you but live as true
As we have done for years;

"Your father thirty years ago
Had just your tale to tell;
But he was not so pale as you,
Nor I so pale as Nell."

My lord was pale with inward strife,
And Nell was pale with pride;
My lord gazed long on pale Maude Clare
Or ever he kissed the bride.

"Lo, I have brought my gift, my lord,
Have brought my gift, " she said:
To bless the hearth, to bless the board,
To bless the marriage-bed.

"Here's my half of the golden chain
You wore about your neck,
That day we waded ankle-deep
For lilies in the beck:

"Here's my half of the faded leaves
We plucked from the budding bough,
With feet amongst the lily leaves, -
The lilies are budding now."

He strove to match her scorn with scorn,
He faltered in his place:
"Lady, " he said, - "Maude Clare, " he said-
"Maude Clare, " – and hid his face.

She turn'd to Nell: "My Lady Nell,
I have a gift for you;
Though, were it fruit, the blooms were gone,
Or, were it flowers, the dew.

"Take my share of a fickle heart,
Mine of a paltry love:
Take it or leave it as you will,
I wash my hands thereof."

"And what you leave, " said Nell, "I'll take,
And what you spurn, I'll wear;
For he's my lord for better and worse,
And him I love Maude Clare.

"Yea, though you're taller by the head,
More wise and much more fair:
I'll love him till he loves me best,
Me best of all Maude Clare.

CONTEXT

- Attitudes towards women and independence
- Rossetti's experiences of love

There's two very different women described here competing for Thomas's affections – and his mother, too. In Rossetti's portrayal, does anyone seem "the one" we should be rooting for?

> **Out of the church she followed them**
> **With a lofty step and mien:**
> **His bride was like a village maid,**
> **Maude Clare was like a queen.**

Using a ballad form, this narrative poem tells the story of Nell and Thomas, newly-weds, who are accosted by Maude Clare as they leave the church who, it emerges, had a relationship with Thomas. The woman is initially simply referred to as "She" – but we can perhaps infer from the title that this is Maude Clare. Throughout there's a question as to who we're supposed to identify with: is it the woman of the title and beginning, or the woman who has the last word? Rossetti immediately contrasts the two women in a way that sets up the conflict of the rest of the poem; Maude Clare is "lofty", superiority in everything about her, while "his bride" isn't even named and is "like a village maid", which sounds quite condescending and patronizing. It's also ironic that a bride would usually, on her wedding day, be the "queenly" woman, so to give this title to someone else implies that there is something wrong here. When first published, this poem was accompanied by an illustration which placed Maude Clare in rich finery in the centre of attention in the middle of a crowd as she accused the couple. There was some discussion at the time over the role of women in marriage, and that with an imbalance of single women there was more competition – yet women weren't supposed to pursue men.

> **"Son Thomas, " his lady mother said,**
> **With smiles, almost with tears:**
> **"May Nell and you but live as true**
> **As we have done for years;**

Thomas's mother is suitably emotional for a wedding day and her blessing is quite typical, wishing her son and his bride the happiness she has had with his father. That she is "almost with tears" seems on a first reading natural – what mothers don't cry at weddings?! But then again, is she aware that there is something wrong? Her blessing might also be a way to comfort Nell if she knows how her son truly feels, and to reassure them both.

> **"Your father thirty years ago**
> **Had just your tale to tell;**
> **But he was not so pale as you,**
> **Nor I so pale as Nell."**

This stanza further introduces doubt when Thomas's mother points out that the couple are "pale", and unexpectedly so – what could be causing it? Immediately there seems to be something wrong, particularly with the use of "but" and "nor" indicating the unlikely nature of their appearance. This comment about the father is also interesting, implying that the mother and father's relationship, too, might not have been ideal when they married, but that they are now very happy and so can Thomas and Nell be.

> **My lord was pale with inward strife,**
> **And Nell was pale with pride;**
> **My lord gazed long on pale Maude Clare**
> **Or ever he kissed the bride.**

Is the "my lord" here mocking Thomas? The speaker, after all, knows what is about to happen. The paleness of the two is picked up on as well; while Nell is "pale with pride" – also ironic maybe given the story of the ballad – Thomas is "pale with inward strife." It almost seems like there's a tone of glee here, that Thomas is going to get what he deserves. Maude Clare, too, is pale – but here is the paleness a sign of prettiness, of anger, or something else? The second couplet – "My lord gazed long on pale Maude Clare/Or ever he kissed the bride" is a play on the idea. While it could imply she's interrupted at the perfect moment, just as they were about to kiss in front of the church, it also tells us that he gazed on her *before* he was in a relationship with Nell.

> **"Lo, I have brought my gift, my lord,**
> **Have brought my gift, " she said:**
> **To bless the hearth, to bless the board,**
> **To bless the marriage-bed.**

The repetition of "brought my gift" almost brings to mind a fairytale, suited to the ballad narrative – it feels more like the wicked fairy's curse! Calling him "my lord" seems a little mocking, and although it places her in a slightly subservient position she's about to dramatically challenge him in front of his bride and their families. The triadic anaphora "to bless the hearth/board/marriage bed" also has fairytale qualities to it, but sounds more like a curse than a blessing. The "hearth" symbolizes the warmth and comfort of the couple's future home, It represents their future happiness and wellbeing, is the centre of their house. The "board" refers to the dining table (meals were often served on the *sideboard* as we now call it): Maude Clare is 'blessing' the family's togetherness. Finally, by blessing the marriage bed, Maude Clare is inserting herself between the couple – they'll never be able to enjoy the marriage bed without her blessing and reminder of her. The ironic tone of "blessing" these three essential places puts Maude Clare at the centre of Thomas and Nell's relationship, casting a shadow over every facet of it.

> **"Here's my half of the golden chain**
> **You wore about your neck,**

That day we waded ankle-deep
For lilies in the beck

Here, we reach Maude Clare's reasons for being there – the "golden chain" has
evidently been shared between them, a lover's promise. It seems through the poem that
their relationship was in secret, but didn't stop Maude Clare believing that there might
be more to it. Especially considering Victorian expectations of relationships, this is
essential. There's an interesting contrast between the "golden chain" and wading "for
lilies in the beck" – both romanticised, intimate images, but the difference between the
wealth of the chain and the beautiful natural imagery of the lilies provides a suggestion of
how all-encompassing Maude Clare saw the relationship. She is also implying that
Thomas still has the other half – she's returning hers so it can be whole again.
Considering again Victorian expectations of propriety, "wading" together could be
considered potentially scandalous, including removal of shoes and stockings, raising skirts
and so on.

"Here's my half of the faded leaves
We plucked from the budding bough,
With feet amongst the lily leaves, -
The lilies are budding now."

The symbolism of different flowers was well-established in Victorian England. Lilies are
white, pure and also frequent wedding flowers, used to symbolize fertility. By suggesting
that they're now "budding", Maude Clare casts an ironic comment on Thomas's wedding
day, and suggests her own earlier hopes of marriage. They walked together among the
lilies, and so she brings the idea of the two of them together. The leaves gathered,
though, were already "faded" when the pair picked them which might be an
acknowledgement of the futility of this relationship but also blames Thomas for allowing
her to focus on the "budding bough" instead.

He strove to match her scorn with scorn,
He faltered in his place:
"Lady, " he said, - "Maude Clare, " he said-
"Maude Clare, " – and hid his face.

Thomas is unable to argue with her – he barely manages to speak, never mind "match
her scorn with scorn". Instead he falters and stammers. Hardly the strong patriarchal
authority figure he's supposed to be! Whereas Maude Clare continues to be hold herself
as regal, authoritative and righteous, Thomas is a stumbling child in comparison, who
seems by his halting speech to know he has done wrong and be unable to justify himself.
We have to ask – when did he break it off with Maude Clare? Or, indeed, has he? Hiding

his face is also a childish gesture, as though he can hide from what he's done and the situation he's in by simply refusing to acknowledge it. Here, think about Rossetti's experience with fallen women at the penitentiary (see context, later). She came across so many women who had believed men and then, when they were in trouble, had been abandoned – while she didn't absolve women, who had known what they were doing was wrong, she also believed men too were responsible for their predicament and should be held to account.

> **She turn'd to Nell: "My Lady Nell,**
> **I have a gift for you;**
> **Though, were it fruit, the blooms were gone,**
> **Or, were it flowers, the dew.**

Addressing Nell as "My Lady" should be a mark of respect, but how could we not hear the sarcasm dripping from Maude Clare's voice here? The "gift" being designated for her implies that, so far, the blessings and gifts have been for Thomas alone, although obviously they will affect the marital home and relationship for both of them. Here, the simplicity of the language – "flowers", "fruit" – should have a romantic, joyful impact but they're quickly ruined. Giving her the freshness of fruit and flowers which would be suggestive of fertility is quickly diminished by the comment that the "blooms were gone" along with the dew; all Maude Clare has to offer is old, withered and dying – long past their best.

> **"Take my share of a fickle heart,**
> **Mine of a paltry love:**
> **Take it or leave it as you will,**
> **I wash my hands thereof."**

She claims the ownership of Thomas's "fickle heart" and calls his love "paltry", insulting him but firmly turning her attention to Nell and warning her about his lack of loyalty – adding to the likelihood that the relationships were at the same time. Giving her the choice is almost underhanded at this point as they are already married – they're leaving the church and Maude Clare *could* have spoken up earlier. Her choice to leave her warning until later therefore appears a deliberate act to punish the couple. The final line of the stanza – "I wash my hand thereof" – is Maude Clare's final line, a defiant and angry comment.

> **"And what you leave, " said Nell, "I'll take,**
> **And what you spurn, I'll wear;**
> **For he's my lord for better and worse,**
> **And him I love Maude Clare.**

Although following the last stanza we might expect Nell to be cowed, or intimidated, by Maude Clare's angry revelations, the woman who steps forward to speak next is Nell is defiant – "for better and worse", part of the marriage vows she has just spoken, seem to be true for her. Her syndetic triad - "and what you leave / and what you spurn / and him I love" – speaks of anger, and it seems that either she already knew about Maude Clare's relationship or is proud enough to not let the revelation upset her. Using "leave" and "take" also suggests she knows others might see her as a second choice, but her love for Thomas means she doesn't care. The inversion "And **him** I love" puts the rhythm's emphasis on Thomas, just as Nell is doing.

> **"Yea, though you're taller by the head,**
> **More wise and much more fair:**
> **I'll love him till he loves me best,**
> **Me best of all Maude Clare.**

Nell acknowledges Maude Clare's qualities – tall, graceful, beautiful – but also that she has 'won' Thomas. Her last two lines, with their emphatic repetition "Me best" reminds Maude Clare that she is the one who's married and that, eventually, Thomas will love her – more importantly, he has made the choice of her instead. The reader's left at the end with a strange ambiguity; Nell isn't the weak second-best we might expect but is defiant that she is victorious in this competition. Yet is Rossetti suggesting the competition is worth fighting, or are we supposed to pity Nell for her misguided sense of victory – is Thomas a prize worth winning? Yet by giving her the last words and positioning Maude Clare as the silent onlooker again, is Rossetti implying that women who conform to feminine expectations can expect to succeed in the marriage game?

STRUCTURE AND FORM

Ballad form: The poem uses the ballad form, but with some differences – an abcb rhyme scheme instead of the usual abab. It has a similar rhythm, and tells a story. It's written in 12 quatrains, with a generally linear narrative but the interjection of Maude Clare brings the past to the forefront as she describes their previous relationship.

Rhythm and rhyme are both regular, adding to the story-like qualities of the poem, and its spoken-sounding nature.

CRITICAL INTERPRETATIONS

Christina Rossetti's "Maude Clare" engages in a discourse on hegemonic definitions of Victorian femininity. This issue is dealt with on multiple layers which in turn either reinforce or challenge these gendered ideals in their reflections on the position of women. The illustration in combination with the text as well as the layout challenge these ideals, however the explicit and implicit meanings of the text itself lessen this challenge and create a more ambiguous position. Perhaps this ambiguity is more reflective on the actual position of women at the time however as the demographics in the population made it impossible for all women to accomplish the goals set for them by society, placing them in an ambiguous position indeed.

Victorian Femininity in "Maude Clare", Andrew Stewart and Alexandra Russel

CONNECTIONS

Male and female relationships: No Thank You John; Shut Out; Soeur Louise
Imagery of Nature: Shut Out; Birthday; Remember
Love: No Thank You John; Remember; Song; Goblin Market
Narrative form: Goblin Market

Millais's illustration of *Maude Clare* for its publication in *Once a Week*

[1]I never said I loved you, John:
Why will you tease me day by day,
And wax a weariness to think upon
With always "do" and "pray"?

[5]You Know I never loved you, John;
No fault of mine made me your toast:
Why will you haunt me with a face as
wan
As shows an hour-old ghost?

I dare say Meg or Moll would take
[10]Pity upon you, if you'd ask:
And pray don't remain single for my
sake
Who can't perform the task.

I have no heart?-Perhaps I have not;
But then you're mad to take offence
[15]That I don't give you what I have not
got:
Use your common sense.

Let bygones be bygones:
Don't call me false, who owed not to
be true:
I'd rather answer "No" to fifty Johns
[20]Than answer "Yes" to you.

Let's mar our pleasant days no more,
Song-birds of passage, days of youth:
Catch at today, forget the days before:
I'll wink at your untruth.

[25]Let us strike hands as hearty friends;
No more, no less; and friendship's
good:
Only don't keep in view ulterior ends,
And points not understood

In open treaty. Rise above
[30]Quibbles and shuffling off and on:
Here's friendship for you if you like;
but love,-
No, thank you, John.

CONTEXT:

- Role of women, in particular with regard to marriage
- Women's independence and authority
- Opinions of love

INTERPRETATION / ANALYSIS

I never said I loved you, John:
Why will you tease me day by day,
And wax a weariness to think upon
With always "do" and "pray"?

Rossetti's speaker begins her dramatic monologue with a refutation to the unheard
listener – like *Winter: My Secret*, the speaker is both playful and coy, while holding her
ground steadfastly. The bluntness of the first line is contrary to what is often seen as the
Victorian feminine ideal, meek and submissive – but in Rossetti's own life, she clearly

held the view that remaining unmarried was better than being unhappily married (and, happily, had the financial independence to enable her to remain single). The man is "teasing", a word often reserved for women, but in his persistence is also infuriating – does he see it as his right to marry and think, as Mr Collins does in Austen's *Pride and Prejudice*, that is it simply a matter of wooing, a game of flirtation and romance? Rossetti's speaker emphasizes her irritation with the alliterative "wax a weariness" and the "do and pray" indicates his persistence in persuading her – those imperatives are commanding her: but she will not be commanded.

As I must therefore conclude that you are not serious in your rejection of me, I shall chuse to attribute it to your wish of increasing my love by suspense, according to the usual practice of elegant females. (Mr Collins Pride and Prejudice)

> **You Know I never loved you, John;**
> **No fault of mine made me your toast:**
> **Why will you haunt me with a face as wan**
> **As shows an hour-old ghost?**

The frustration and assertiveness grows – perhaps a response to the listener –in "you **know**", refusing to give any ground. The interesting second line "no fault of mine" also suggests a disgust with social conventions assuming that women 'lead on' or 'entrap' men in some way – how little has changed! The suggestion that women are no matter what to blame for men's feelings is strongly refuted. This is an extremely confident woman who is not only refusing her suitor, but forcing him to see the truth of his situation rather than blame her. Her language becomes harsh and insulting – "haunting", "ghost" – to force him to stay away. Maybe there is also a touch of concern here; will her decision continue to haunt her beyond her refusal, given Victorian roles of women and social expectation?

> **I dare say Meg or Moll would take**
> **Pity upon you, if you'd ask:**
> **And pray don't remain single for my sake**
> **Who can't perform the task.**

The "I dare say" carries a touch more bitterness, maybe that the listener continues to argue back, and the language becomes harsher still. The husband would be taken for "pity" not for love, emphasized at the beginning of the line. The alliterative choice of "Meg or Moll" draws attention to the names yet at the same time makes them the same; there is no reason to distinguish between these second-choice girls, they are all the same for his purposes – as perhaps is she, in the end, for there is little to suggest she believes he genuinely loves her. Her choice of "can't perform" is also interesting as there is often in Victorian literature a suggestion that love can be learned, or will come later –

and is indeed the basis of many arranged marriages — but the speaker refutes that suggestion. Marriage is a "task" to be performed, a chore rather than a joyful blessing.

> I have no heart?-Perhaps I have not;
> But then you're mad to take offence
> That I don't give you what I have not got:
> Use your common sense.

The starting rhetorical question implies she's repeating an accusation thrown at her by the speaker in his increasing anger. Her following wordplay — "you're mad to take offence /That I don't give you what I have not got" — shows that she still retrains an element of humour about the situation, although it's now more sarcastic and frustrated with him.

She's blunt — he is "mad" and the single-line imperative "use your common sense" almost puts him in the place of a child being scolded rather than an equal. However, she remains firm: she doesn't have love to give him and therefore will not marry him.

There is an echo too of Jane Eyre's refusal of St. John Rivers who suggests "enough of love will follow" their marriage, to which she replies: "I scorn your idea of love...I scorn the counterfeit sentiment you offer, and I scorn you when you offer it."

> Let bygones be bygones:
> Don't call me false, who owed not to be true:
> I'd rather answer "No" to fifty Johns
> Than answer "Yes" to you.

The tone becomes briefly more conciliatory here — she wishes him to allow her the choice. Throughout she's still insistent she's never been "false" — there's a definite anger here that she is expected to simply acquiesce to his request for a relationship. But her friendly first line is quickly lost with the sarcastic "I'd rather answer no to fifty Johns" She is determined, no matter how persistent he may be, to refuse his proposal. His accusation of betrayal is, too, soundly refuted. The speaker is not content with refusing but she will insist that this relationship has been created by him with no input from her, "who owed not to be true."

> Let's mar our pleasant days no more,
> Song-birds of passage, days of youth:
> Catch at today, forget the days before:
> I'll wink at your untruth.

Yet in this stanza she seems to tire of arguing and agrees to "wink at your untruth" - agree to disagree, yet we both know it is an "untruth". The introduction of sweeter imagery – "song-birds", "days of youth", "pleasant days" are vaguely lovely, though unspecific, but they are an indication that life is too short to spend arguing and bearing a grudge. "Catch at today" encourages him to move on from her, and spend his time in more pleasant pursuits.

> **Let us strike hands as hearty friends;**
> **No more, no less; and friendship's good:**
> **Only don't keep in view ulterior ends,**
> **And points not understood**
>
> **In open treaty. Rise above**
> **Quibbles and shuffling off and on:**
> **Here's friendship for you if you like; but love,-**
> **No, thank you, John.**

Even in parting she warns that this is no ploy – "don't keep in view ulterior ends/and points not understood//in open treaty." The language of conciliation in war implies her firmness; the "treaty" should bring peace, if both parties abide by it. "Hearty friends" is generous, and shows her willingness to continue her association yet she will not brook marriage or love. "No more, no less, and friendship's good" – there is value in being good friends, and unusually for a Victorian writer Rossetti acknowledges the value of friends of the opposite sex who were, of course, quite difficult to continue given the social expectations. She appeals to his pride too – "rise above/quibbles" – the word "quibble" making it seem petty and childish again. She offers generously "here's friendship for you if you like" but then leaves the decision to him. The finality of the last line, the cyclical echo of the beginning's direct address reminds us of her determination, and that she has not changed her stance since the beginning. Marriage, with John at least, is not for her.

Structure and Form

- **Repeated rhythmic structure** in each stanza, perhaps to reflect the tedium of having to resist this suitor over and over.
- **Enjambment of the final two stanzas.** The majority of stanzas stand alone with the exception of the final two, where the speaker tries finally to appease John and encourage him to accept friendship instead of love – the enjambment here makes the stanzas a little less blunt, less harsh, as she takes a softer tone.
- **Regular rhyme** also frequently highlights her bluntness, ending lines on harsh consonants or the particularly language of denial.
- As a **dramatic monologue** the speaker is clearly addressing "John" – Rossetti sometimes creates these specific characters to attempt to portray different

viewpoints, perhaps to give herself more freedom than she might have in her own voice.

"She seems to write directly and bitterly to one of her suitors…To reject a marriage proposal seemed counter to the Victorian mentality, and for Rossetti to assert herself in such as way as she does in this poem adds to her character a sense of strength and profound assertiveness which Virginia Woolf touches upon in her essay about Rossetti. Woolf says that once at a tea party, Rossetti overheard someone say something negative about poetry in a "casual, frivolous, tea-party way" (Woolf). Rossetti promptly stood up from her seat at the table, marched directly to the centre of the room and declared fervently, "I am Christina Rossetti!" (Woolf). This is a move that, though somewhat ambiguous to us today, I take as being symbolic of her strong sensibilities about life. In "No, Thank You, John," Rossetti seems to repeat what she said that day at the tea party. She goes on in the poem to encourage the rejected suitor to pursue other women, saying: I dare say Meg or Moll would take Pity upon you, if you'd ask: And pray don't remain single for my sake Who can't perform that task. Rossetti effortlessly and sharply convinces her audience that she is a woman whom the conventions of society could not shake in any area; that she had her own agenda in life."

The Possibilities of Interpretation in Christina Rossetti's "Goblin Market"
Gaynell Galt

In his Family Letters of Christina Rossetti (1908) William Michael writes 'Yet John was not absolutely mythical for, in one of her volumes which I possess, Christina made a pencil jotting, 'The original John was obnoxious because he never gave scope for 'No, thank you'. This John was, I am sure the marine painter John Brett who (at a date long antecedent, say 1852) had appeared to be somewhat smitten with Christina…' William Michael may have had the dates wrong and it could be a later relationship, but Dante also tried to dissuade Christina from including the poem writing to her it was '"utterly foreign to your primary impulses' (Letters III, 1380)".

CONNECTIONS

Women's difficulties in society –Winter: My Secret; Shut Out; Soeur Louise; Maude Clare; From the Antique
Playful, almost ironic tone: Winter: My Secret; Maude Clare
Love: Twice; Goblin Market Maude Clare

[1]Remember me when I am gone away,
Gone far away into the silent land;
When you can no more hold me by the hand,
Nor I half turn to go yet turning stay.
[5]Remember me when no more day by day
You tell me of our future that you planned:
Only remember me; you understand
It will be late to counsel then or pray.
Yet if you should forget me for a while
[10]And afterwards remember, do not grieve:
For if the darkness and corruption leave
A vestige of the thoughts that once I had,
Better by far you should forget and smile
Than that you should remember and be sad.

CONTEXT

Victorians had strict rules and interpretations of grief. There were specific social conventions for what colours and fabrics to wear, and for how long, to honour the dead, depending on the closeness of your relationship with them. Because death was such a common part of life, including high infant mortality and frequent deaths from illnesses we'd now be able to treat relatively easily, Victorians became quite superstitious about death and grieving. After the invention of the camera, photographs of the dead were taken, for example, and were - often the only photograph that person would have.

- Religious beliefs in the afterlife
- Rossetti's romantic experiences

INTERPRETATION / ANALYSIS

This sonnet is a partner to *Song (When I am Dead)* in many ways. Both explore memory and the afterlife, and the responsibilities for grief from those left behind. Despite Rossetti's Christian belief in the afterlife, there is still a conflict to be resolved between that faith and the natural grief occurring when losing a loved one. This poem is from the perspective of the dying, rather than the one left behind. Rossetti's speaker begins the sonnet with an imperative to "remember", and the description of the afterlife as a "silent land" which isn't a very optimistic viewpoint, but is similar to that in *Song* when she describes the silent dream. "Silent" and the lack of communication later in the poem might also be a reference to Rossetti's belief in soul sleep, the silent dreamless state souls enter after death and before the end of the world.

The instruction to "remember" is repeated through the poem, but becomes more of a discussion of the value of memory instead; is it something the lover should strive to do if it makes them unhappy? The direct address "you" throughout indicates the personal, intimate nature of this poem. Repeating "gone away" / "gone far away" emphasizes the boundary of life and death, symbolized elsewhere in the collection by a door or wall; here it is characterized as a different country.

The second couplet "When you can...yet turning stay" holds echoes of the Greek myth of Orpheus, who tried to rescue his wife Eurydice from the underworld but turned around as they were leaving to see her, breaking the spell and dooming her to final death. The speaker here can't communicate, can't hold hands or contemplate a future with their lover. The speaker, however, can be seen as quite demanding (especially by modern standards) when they instruct "Only remember me", the "only" at the beginning of the line emphasizing the futility of trying to do anything else. The caesura after this phrase allows the listener time to remember, before she gently reminds them it's too late to "counsel of pray" – neither will have any effect now. This is a darker version of the afterlife again, one which doesn't admit the ability of those on earth to pray, or intercede for the dead. Once dead, they must await judgement and the afterlife they have earned.

At the volta (line 9) the speaker relents and changes idea, granting forgiveness to the listener for moving on and forgetting her: "do not grieve." Again, the afterlife is portrayed as damaging, with "darkness and corruption" removing even the final thoughts of her.

The final couple, with its parallels "forget and smile" / "remember and be sad", are a benediction, a wish for her lover's future happiness even at the expense of her own memory.

STRUCTURE AND FORM

- **Sonnet form** Rossetti uses a Petrarchan sonnet, with its connotations of a love poem, and she adheres strictly to the rhyme scheme and the overall structure. She uses an octave (eight lines) then has the volta (change of idea) – "Yet if you should forget me" when she begins to give permission to the lover to move on.

- **Change in idea** as well as the volta's change, giving permission for the lover to forget, the tone becomes more tentative throughout the poem as Rossetti shifts from the imperative "remember" to the conditional "yet if you should forget"
- **Rhyme –** Rossetti uses the Petrarchan convention (abba, abba, cddece) but the disruption of the sestet (last six lines) suggests the emotion of the speaker
- **Iambic pentameter** – as well as being a convention of the sonnet, the iambic rhythm highlights important words; however, there's a slight disruption at line 7 where the tendency reading aloud is to invert the first two syllables "**on**ly" which highlights the volta, and the hesitation of the speaker as she's giving her lover permission to forget her.

CRITICAL INTERPRETATIONS

Christina Rossetti fell in love twice in her life. The first time with James Collinson. then later with Charles Cayley. The paradoxical character of Christina's genius when she was in love can be seen from the poems which she then wrote. None of her poems to Collinson reflects joy or hope. On the contrary, at the height of her love for him she wrote some of her most poignant lines on the imminence and the pathos of death. In her the idea of love turned inexorably to the idea of death, and in this association we can surely see her instinctive shrinking from the surrender which love demands. Two of her most famous poems come from this time, and in each Christina is obsessed by thoughts of death. In "Remember" she asks her beloved to remember her when she is dead, because that is all that he will be able to do for her. Then, with characteristic humility, she assures him that even this is not necessary and that all she asks is that he himself should not be unhappy.

> Yet if you should forget me for awhile
> And afterwards remember, do not grieve:
> For if the darkness and corruption leave
> A vestige of the thoughts that I once had,
> Better by far you should forget and smile
> Than that you should remember and be sad.

In the wonderful "Song" which is a kind of counterpart to this sonnet, Christina foresees what death will mean to her and wonders if perhaps she also will forget the past:

> I shall not see the shadows,
> I shall not feel the rain;
> I shall not hear the nightingale
> Sing on as if in pain;
> And dreaming through the twilight
> That doth not rise nor set,

Haply I may remember,
And haply I may forget.

In Rossetti, love released a melancholy desire for death, and for a kind of death not closely connected with her usual ideas of an afterworld. It is an intermediate condition between sleeping and waking, a half-conscious state in which memories are dim and even the strongest affections fade into shadows. Moreover, she felt that the claims of love were not for her, that her way of life was unsuited to it, and that she must go back to her old denials and refusals.

Rigorous though Christina's denial of love was, it was not strong enough to curb all her womanly and human instincts. She fought against them and kept them in iron control, but, left alone with her genius, she could not from time to time prevent them from bursting into almost heart-rending poetry, which is all the more powerful because it rises not from controlled thoughts but from longings which force themselves on her despite all her efforts to check them. It is not surprising that, being the victim of such a struggle, she sometimes felt it was too much for her and she could not bear it endure longer. At such times she would long for release and find no magic even in the spring;

I wish I were dead, my foe,
My friend, I wish I were dead,
With a stone at my tired feet
With a stone at my head.

In the pleasant April days
Half the world will stir and sing,
But half the world will slug and rot
For all the sap of Spring.

In these words there is more than a passing mood: there is a deep basis of experience, of misery in a defeat which has been hard for Christina to endure."

Bowra, C. M. *The Romantic Imagination*. Cambridge: Harvard UP, 1949.

CONNECTIONS

Death and the afterlife: Song; From the Antique; Twice; Echo; Birthday; Uphill
Love and memory: Song; Echo; Shut-Out

The door was shut. I looked between
Its iron bars; and saw it lie,
My garden, mine, beneath the sky,
Pied with all flowers bedewed and green:

From bough to bough the song-birds crossed,
From flower to flower the moths and bees;
With all its nests and stately trees
It had been mine, and it was lost.

A shadowless spirit kept the gate,
Blank and unchanging like the grave.
I peering through said: 'Let me have
Some buds to cheer my outcast state.'

He answered not. 'Or give me, then,
But one small twig from shrub or tree;
And bid my home remember me
Until I come to it again.'

The spirit was silent; but he took
Mortar and stone to build a wall;
He left no loophole great or small
Through which my straining eyes might look:

So now I sit here quite alone
Blinded with tears; nor grieve for that,
For nought is left worth looking at
Since my delightful land is gone.

A violet bed is budding near,
Wherein a lark has made her nest:
And good they are, but not the best;
And dear they are, but not so dear

CONTEXT:

- Rossetti's religious beliefs and life
- Rossetti's family and romantic experiences
- Roles of women in Victorian society
- The original sub-title while writing was "What happened to me"

INTERPRETATION / ANALYSIS

The door was shut. I looked between
Its iron bars; and saw it lie,
My garden, mine, beneath the sky,
Pied with all flowers bedewed and green:

The blunt short sentence "the door was shut" with its mid-line caesura sets the tone for the rest of the poem; whether interpreted as religious allegory or a commentary on female life in some way (see later) the finality of that sentence implies that there is no hope for the future. The "iron bars", man-made, cold and hard objects which keep her out of the natural garden which the speaker goes on to describe. Imagery of the door is frequent in Rossetti's collection, usually indicating a barrier between life and death, a liminal space to be crossed.

The garden in this poem could be interpreted quite easily as the religious allegory of Eden, with the (likely) female speaker being locked out as a result of Eve's fall and female subsequent loss of innocence. However, there is a multiplicity of interpretation and this can be a very flexible poem in terms of theme. It can be seen as symbolic of Rossetti's own exclusion from life's pleasures; the speaker perhaps lamenting the loss of a relationship – it was written shortly after Rossetti's ended relationship with Collinson over their religious differences – or it could be a struggle to come to terms with the need for self-denial that Rossetti seemingly felt throughout her life.

The possessive repetition of "my garden, mine", which is emphasized by the rhythm, shows us how melancholy the speaker is about the loss of it, but there's also a tone of anger or recrimination at being kept out of something she feels is her rightful place. The "sky" and "flowers bedewed and green" is a colourful, calm image in stark contrast with the iron bars excluding her.

Caesura through the first three lines represents the difficulty of the speaker, and the lock-out of the speaker. The lack of caesura on line 4 suggests a contrasting ease within the garden it describes.

> **From bough to bough the song-birds crossed,**
> **From flower to flower the moths and bees;**
> **With all its nests and stately trees**
> **It had been mine, and it was lost.**

The repeated stressed phrases "bough to bough", "flower to flower", continue this calm and peaceful image, a sing-song rhythm being established alongside the assonance of these phrases, again a lengthening quality suggesting longing. The overwhelming sense of nature extends to the animals, too – the "song-birds", "moths and bees" – the perhaps odd addition of the moth, usually associated with darkness or decay, instead here contributes to the sense of peace, quiet – they're less showy than their butterfly counterpart, and it suggests softness. The "nest" and "trees" create a similar sense of inclusion – the garden is for all stages of life, which makes her lack of entry even more frustrating and devastating to contemplate.

Internal rhyme here (Crossed, moths, for example) shows the connections within the garden; all life there is continuous and works together, co-existing in harmony. It is only the speaker who is left outside. The final line reveals her loss, again with the juxtaposition of "mine" indicating her possessive anger, its caesura making the last "it was lost" sound even more despairing.

A shadowless spirit kept the gate,
Blank and unchanging like the grave.
I peering through said: 'Let me have
Some buds to cheer my outcast state.'

In "shadowless spirit", the sibilance creates a tone of mystery, eerie as the shadow that crosses the gate in front of her. Here we have the first reference to death, the "Blank and unchanging" grave. The speaker can only "peer" through the iron bars. There isn't enough space for her to see properly, or get a clear look. When she pleads with the spirit to give her some comfort – "buds to cheer my outcast state" – she asks for very little, but is refused. The harsh sound of the words here – "blank", "grave", "outcaste state" – echo the despair she is feeling and the coldness of life outside the garden. She must ask permission – "Let me have" – and has to entirely hand over her happiness to the silent stranger. Here it seems as though she is hopeful there may be some resolution – her "outcast state" can be cheered, suggesting that she might be permitted back in again.

The spirit could be interpreted as God, or Jesus however it is an unusually cold response, though this suits the religious doubt Rossetti often explores – faith without any proof. It could also be a former lover, if the speaker wants to resume a relationship, or even (see Critical Interpretations, below) a family member who's died, and the speaker wishes reassurance from them.

This could also be a poem about childlessness and lack of family life. Although Rossetti never married or had children, she remained close to her brother's children and the children pf her former fiancé, and it seems that she found these relationships fulfilling, although the "peering through" could imply that she's aware of her role always on the periphery of this family experience. This, in addition to the social expectations of women, could possibly have made her own lack of children quite difficult to bear.

He answered not. 'Or give me, then,
But one small twig from shrub or tree;
And bid my home remember me
Until I come to it again.'

She is completely ignored, perhaps a comment on Rossetti's religious doubt and the lack of God's voice speaking directly. She lessens her request – instead of a bud from which can come new growth, life, she asks instead for "one small twig", something from which no more life can come but which can serve as a reminder. That the speaker is male also gives him authority, and lends weight to the religious interpretation. Is it possible to read this as women being shut out of the world, kept out of the "garden" of life through male authority? Given Rossetti's personal views on women's roles, it seems a perhaps unlikely interpretation but certainly can be read this way.

Once more she calls the garden "home", which supports the allegory of this being about religion and the Garden of Eden, or heaven. The sense of exclusion grows even stronger.

> **The spirit was silent; but he took**
> **Mortar and stone to build a wall;**
> **He left no loophole great or small**
> **Through which my straining eyes might look**:

Here we see a note of cruelty from inside the garden – not only "silent" and ignoring her entirely, the spirit now builds a wall of "mortar and stone", in order to completely exclude her as even the gap in the iron bars is too much for her to be permitted. The "mortar and stone", however, is also man-made, which could be the speaker's allegory referring to the loss of innocence – made by mans' choices – and the ways that men behave on earth, excluding themselves from paradise by their actions. Yet, the speaker is a "spirit" and so this is ambiguous; who is she blaming for her exclusion?

The speaker remains desperate for entry, "straining" to see but to no avail. This barrier is now permanent. Whereas the door has the possibility of opening, there is no such hope for a brick wall, and every loophole has been closed to her. There's far less caesura in this section of the poem; the despair is now overwhelming, and the exclusion more complete as she cannot see into the garden at all.

> **So now I sit here quite alone**
> **Blinded with tears; nor grieve for that,**
> **For nought is left worth looking at**
> **Since my delightful land is gone**.

Here, the speaker changes from past to present tense – "Now I sit here quite alone" – a more resigned tone, having explained how they come to be sitting there. The first line demonstrates her inability to enjoy life with the knowledge of her exclusion, and no hope of its return. The metaphor of sight remains just as important as she's "blinded with tears" but unable to care because there's nothing else worth looking at once she has glimpsed the garden. If we read this as a poem about personal loss and relationships, it's easy to see the misery that can come after the end of a relationship with no hope of reconciliation. However, sight is also frequently referenced in the Bible as either being blinded to the truth or being able to see it, and used as a metaphor for a positive relationship with God – which the speaker now lacks.

A violet bed is budding near,
Wherein a lark has made her nest:
And good they are, but not the best;
And dear they are, but not so dear.

Violets are often associated in Victorian literature with fidelity, and a lark symbolizes hope and possibility. Yet the speaker here doesn't seem as positive as these images might suggest. They are, after all, merely representations and reflections, not the truth of her emotions. The lark is also given a female pronoun, adding to the interpretation of this as being about female roles in society – she is home-making, but it is not good enough. Maybe ironically, the lark has more domestic property than Victorian women, whose husbands owned their property.

The final couplet with its comparative statements gives the conclusive tone: nothing now will be any good. She can appreciate, from a more aesthetic viewpoint, the beauty of the violet and the lark, but they hold no emotional value for her anymore.

STRUCTURE AND FORM

Iambic pentameter reflecting the monotony of the speaker's life, and a common way to write a narrative poem as it echoes rhythm of speech.

Inversion of the iamb on 2nd line, stanzas 3, 5, and 6 to convey the interruption and difficulty of the speaker

ABBA rhyme scheme – while regular, which may seem contradictory given the emotional tone of the poem, it suggests that this decision to shut her out is irreversible

CRITICAL INTERPRETATION

Perhaps this childish tone represents a sense of self-deprivation, of the speaker humbling herself to the spirit, or a sense of deserving this loss inflicted upon her.

This leads to the question of who this speaker is supposed to be, and why she has been 'shut out'. As indicated earlier, there is an obvious separation in this poem, which is possible to interpret as being between earthly and spiritual. This points to a biblical perspective where the garden is the Garden of Eden. Kathleen Jones presents this interpretation, wherein the speaker represents Eve (or in the larger perspective, mankind), while the spirit represents either God or a representation of God in the shape of an angel. This would explain why the speaker has been cast out of the garden, and why she feels that this is justly deserved, and also that she hopes to come back one day, either by repenting her sins and/or being taken into Paradise after her death. It would also explain the idea that no earthly garden can live up to the Paradise that is

Eden, as well as the violets and the lark, representing that she needs to learn humility before God and not desire to be God's equal, like the biblical Eve.

It is easy to imagine that either Eve did feel very lonely once cast out of Paradise with Adam accusing her of tempting him, or mankind is alone on earth in the absence of God. Another possible way to interpret this poem is that, like "Goblin Market", it is a poem about coping with personal loss and temptation, or jealousy. If so, it means to show how the loss of something dear could be devastating. However, the gloominess and generally depressing tone of the poem is more indicative of grieving after loss than coping with jealousy. It is, of course, very befitting the Gothic to leave the happy ending out, and what is clearly visible here is that Rossetti intentionally makes this poem sadder by taking this stanza out, showing how she deviates from an otherwise romantic theme and creates a Gothic tone of her own.

It has also been suggested that this poem was written as a response to the ending of Rossetti's engagement to Collinson and that it is a poem where she mentally works through her emotions over this loss. As Crump shows in her notes, an earlier edition of the poem had the subtitle "What happened to me", confirming that this poem is indeed reflecting on a personal experience (although we cannot be sure which experience). Following this train of thought, Sawtell has interpreted the spirit to be either Frances and Maria, Christina's mother and sister, who did not approve of the relationship, or God splitting the couple up because of Collinson's decision to go back to the Catholic Church.

Waldman argues that "Shut Out" shows representations of a psychoanalytical superego in the character of the spirit. She recognizes this "ego-ideal" to represent God and considering Rossetti's beliefs this is a likely interpretation. Religious ideals are here in conflict with the character's inner desires. The spirit represents authority, and this ego-ideal does not speak or give instructions so the speaker is left with her questions and her hopes of eventually being forgiven, or possibly, of forgiving herself.

The Forgotten Gothic of Christina Rossetti, Lars Wallner

<u>Religious</u>: Remember; Good Friday; Song
<u>Women's roles</u>: Maude Clare; No Thank You John; From the Antique
<u>Relationships</u>: Remember; Twice; Winter: My Secret
<u>Nature</u>: Birthday; Song; Maude Clare

I have desired, and I have been desired;
But now the days are over of desire,
Now dust and dying embers mock my fire;
Where is the hire for which my life was hired?
Oh vanity of vanities, desire!

Longing and love, pangs of a perished pleasure,
Longing and love, a disenkindled fire,
And memory a bottomless gulf of mire,
And love a fount of tears outrunning measure;
Oh vanity of vanities, desire!

Now from my heart, love's deathbed, trickles, trickles,
Drop by drop slowly, drop by drop of fire,
The dross of life, of love, of spent desire;
Alas, my rose of life gone all to prickles,--
Oh vanity of vanities, desire!

Oh vanity of vanities, desire;
Stunting my hope which might have strained up higher,
Turning my garden plot to barren mire;
Oh death-struck love, oh disenkindled fire,
Oh vanity of vanities, desire!

CONTEXT

- Rossetti's ideas about women and sexual desire
- Victorian views on women's roles and behaviour
- Rossetti's religious idealisation

Soeur Louise de Misericorde was originally the French Duchess de la Valliere, at Louis XIV's court. She became his mistress and had several children by him. She caused a great sensation at court when she converted to Catholicism, eventually becoming a nun when she became Soeur Louise. A "misericorde" was originally a knife, a long thin dagger used to grant mercy to injured knights, so her adopted religious name translates as "Sister Louise of mercy." She was also very unusual in that she wrote several religious books, including some that were considered to be so important that some questioned whether she'd written them – apparently they were too good to have been written by a man!

"She emerged as the "Magdalene" of neoclassical France, the model of the penitent who had abandoned the court in favour of the convent."

The Suspicion of Virtue: Women Philosophers in Neoclassical France

(John J. Conley)

"O Lord, glorious God of mercy, change my inconstancy into firmness, change all my disordered passions into a burning thirst for Your charity"
– Mlle de la Valliere, Reflections on the Mercy of God

INTERPRETATION / ANALYSIS

> **I have desired, and I have been desired;**
> **But now the days are over of desire,**
> **Now dust and dying embers mock my fire;**
> **Where is the hire for which my life was hired?**
> **Oh vanity of vanities, desire!**

Rossetti's speaker here is a deliberate character – creating a persona, like that of *Winter: My Secret* or *No, Thank You, John*, but this time creating a voice for a real person. It's possible Rossetti had read some of Soeur Louise's books, as her story does tie in with Rossetti's own religious beliefs, including the elements of conversion and Soeur Louise's expressed desire in later life to turn her back on desire in favour of God's love.

The almost constant repetition of "desire" and "longing" throughout the poem is indicative of Rossetti's attempts to understand and portray Louise's state of mind. The first line is a strong statement of equality – there's no attempts to claim a distance from desire. Rossetti's speakers often own their desire, rather than rejecting it. The alliterative "dust and dying embers" has connotations of the funeral tie "ashes to ashes,

dust to dust" but equally conjures the image of a woman who has spent her life a slave, in some respects, to her passions but as she ages, has come to realise how little desire can bring her. The rhetorical question of the fifth line begins to sound more despairing, too, particularly when

59

followed with the shorter exclamative refrain: "Oh vanity of vanities, desire!" By decrying desire as a "vanity", Rossetti coolly identifies desire as purely selfish, a way for people to feel validated, loved or worthy in being desired. Rossetti's experience of desire must surely have been conflicted – with at least two marriage proposals, and a surprisingly close male friendship with her second suitor (see Context) – as well as of course a teenage girl! – she must have experienced intense desire. Yet with her religious leanings, and her work with the fallen women at the Penitentiary, like many Victorian women she no doubt also felt that this emotion was in some way wrong. She also seems to have found the idea of nuns intriguing (her sister Maria Francesca later joined a sisterhood) as several of her poems feature nun speakers.

While there is a possible interpretation (linked with *Twice*, perhaps) that the fiery desire is the love *for* God, the line "dust and dying embers **mock** my fire" (my emphasis) suggests that this fire was in fact damaging after all, else why would she feel mocked?

> **Longing and love, pangs of a perished pleasure,**
> **Longing and love, a disenkindled fire,**
> **And memory a bottomless gulf of mire,**
> **And love a fount of tears outrunning measure;**
> **Oh vanity of vanities, desire!**

The alliteration of "longing and love", repeated on two lines, elongates the sound here and draws attention to the pleasures of love, aided by the trochee of "longing" interrupting the previously iambic rhythm. Yet the next alliterative phrase with its plosive sound - "pangs of a perished pleasure" - makes these sound almost painful instead. The phrase "disenkindled fire" is repeated in the last stanza. It can sound a little clunky, almost, but the harsh consonants emphasize the difficult nature of desire. Memory is a "bottomless gulf of mire" and love "a fount of tears", both terrible images of dirt and misery which overtake the speaker. The gentle "longing and love" is nothing compared with the harsh, unpleasant imagery at the end of the stanza. These two lines, with the introduction of anapests mid-way through, also continue the disruption of the rhythm, as the speaker's life has been interrupted by her desire. The refrain of the final line once again emphasizes the despairing nature of the poem. The line "vanity of vanities" is drawn from the Bible, this time the book of Job which explores the futility of human activity yet insists that God's laws must be followed.

This poem was originally published in *A Pageant and Other poems* in 1881, when Rossetti was in her early fifties – although the poems weren't *always* written around the time of publication, this would lend weight to this poem as a rumination on aging and the lessening of desire that occurs, particularly when Rossetti has not married.

> **Now from my heart, love's deathbed, trickles, trickles,**
> **Drop by drop slowly, drop by drop of fire,**
> **The dross of life, of love, of spent desire;**
> **Alas, my rose of life gone all to prickles, --**
> **Oh vanity of vanities, desire!**

Linguistically, the semantic field here continues to be of loss – trickle, drop, dross, spent, gone to prickles. The speaker mourns the destruction that her desire has caused, and regrets that her "rose of life" has become thorns instead, painful rather than beautiful. The rhythmic pace here is slowed down as well; a combination of iambs, anapests and trochees means that it's sometimes difficult to take hold of – perhaps either like the desire itself, acknowledging the futility of trying to control it, or like the loss it has caused. All that is left now is the "dross", what is left from a material once it's burned up and used.

Desire, repeated over and over, is blamed for having destroyed both life and love. The heart is "love's deathbed", a startlingly bleak image in contradiction to the usual clichés pf the heart and love. This stanza lingers again; the long first line, for example. Then, the slow pace of phrase like "drop by drop", repeats to elongate the line and draw out the life-in-death quality of the poem; is Rossetti's speaker *entirely* wishing she had never felt desire – is there any suggestion that she wishes she *still* felt desire? There is a potential reading, with the "drop by drop of fire" in particular, that the fire of desire may have burned her up and is now "spent" – but wasn't it wonderful to feel something? However, this is quickly negated elsewhere, and Rossetti would never have publicly owned such an interpretation.

> **Oh vanity of vanities, desire;**
> **Stunting my hope which might have strained up higher,**
> **Turning my garden plot to barren mire;**
> **Oh death-struck love, oh disenkindled fire,**
> **Oh vanity of vanities, desire!**

Here, the refrain is also repeated at the *beginning* of the stanza, which means it's read twice in a row – the final amping up of the tone of regret and despair. Her hope is "stunted", and Rossetti uses the familiar image of the garden. Here, the garden is "barren mire" – the "mire" echoed from stanza two – where nothing can grow. It's an irony, perhaps, that the fertility that would accompany desire is no longer there, which is potentially a comment on aging and changing desires. The language "barren" with its connotations of loss of fertility, perhaps also speaks to Rossetti's regret over her childlessness. In other poetry the garden (*Shut Out*, for example) is symbolic of Eden or Heaven. If this is the case here, the imagery implies that Soeur Louise feels that despite her conversion, the garden is closed to her. This seems a harsh interpretation which wouldn't necessarily be fitting with Rossetti's branch of Christianity – the conversion and subsequent moral behaviour would have been weighed in the balance too – but there is always a note of doubt in Rossetti's religious work as to whether her speakers can be good *enough* for Heaven.

Repeated here too is the idea of "death-struck love", linking to the previous stanza's "love's deathbed", connecting the two so closely as to suggest that love has died. It's unclear, though, whether love has died *because* of desire – it's too impure, not able to withstand the fires of desire that have eroded it - or is love ended now that desire has gone because they are so intertwined one cannot survive without the other? The second interpretation would be a more generous, sympathetic one. The phrase "disenkindled fire" is also here again, reiterating that the fire has now gone out and, without desire as a troublesome urge, Louise is able to see the truth of the damage it has wrought on her life, and exclaim the despairing refrain one final time.

STRUCTURE AND FORM

Iambic rhythm in the first stanza creating a natural pace and forward movement which suggests desire may actually be inevitable.

Disruption in the rhythm particularly "longing and love", and "trickles, trickles", "drop by drop" which lengthen and slow the pace, suggesting the speaker lingering over the memory of desire and love.

Rhyme scheme – ABBAB throughout. The final fifth line, the refrain disrupts the regular formality of the poem with its additional B rhyme, just as desire has disrupted Louise's life. Elsewhere in the poem, internal and crossed rhyme draws attention to key words: desire, love, fire.

Repetition – key phrases are repeated, including the refrain highlighting Louise's anguish. "Longing and love", "disenkindled fire" and "mire" are also repeated, showing the depths of the destruction caused by desire.

CRITICAL INTERPRETATION

Of all the poems in the collection for OCR, this is perhaps the least examined critically. When it is explored, it tends to be considered in a sequence with Rossetti's other poems featuring nun speakers (despite the fact that this is the only one of these which names a specific character, the others are generic). In these poems, Rossetti explores the solitary nature of nuns and the way this affects them, but despite some critics' attempts to put them in a sequence, there is no clear cut progression. In some, Rossetti explores isolation as a rejection of the world which renders the woman as good as dead, a pre-death suicide in cutting herself off from everything in the world. In other poems, life in a convent is a respite from the suffering and disaster of the world. In *Convent*

Threshold she explores the difficulty of a nun giving up earthly love in favor of a heavenly love, delayed.

Rossetti wrote in *Seek and Find* that the Biblical line "vanity of vanities":

"Amounts to so exquisite a dirge over dead hope and paralyzed effort that we are almost ready to fall in love with our own desolation and…to drift through life without disquietude."

This possibly applies to the poem's repeated refrain, and can be used to explore Rossetti's interpretation of the futility of desire.

Rosenblum, addressing another of Rossetti's convent-based poems, suggests that the cloister is the adult counterpart of the childhood garden – in *Soeur Louise*, both are destroyed by female desire, reduced to barrenness.

By the time the nun makes her last appearance in *Soeur Louise de la Miseridorde*, renunciation is perfectly stylized, if not perfunctory. This poem is a litany of the language of desire. A limited number of phrases and images are distributed over the three stanzas n a predictable design, each stanza ending with a didactic refrain: O vanity of vanities, desire". The poem echoes the polarities of *The Convent Threshold*: desire is a "disenkindled fire", memory a "bottomless gulf of mire" and desire turned her garden lot to "barren mire". This nun does not mount in the spirit's fire for fire-drops of life's "dross" trickle from her heart. She is being burnt out, to what is really irreducible: the few words that count and that can be repeated endlessly – desire, fire, mire, vanity of vanities.

Christina Rossetti: The Poetry of Endurance
Dolores Rosenblum

CONNECTIONS

- Women's desire and longing (Goblin Market, No, Thank You, John, From the Antique, Winter: My Secret)
- Imagery of the garden and nature (*Shut Out; Goblin Market*)
- Religious and earthly love (*Twice, Good Friday, Shut Out*)

When I am dead, my dearest,
Sing no sad songs for me;
Plant thou no roses at my head,
Nor shady cypress tree:
Be the green grass above me
With showers and dewdrops wet;
And if thou wilt, remember,
And if thou wilt, forget.

I shall not see the shadows,
I shall not feel the rain;
I shall not hear the nightingale
Sing on, as if in pain:
And dreaming through the twilight
That doth not rise nor set,
Haply I may remember,
¹⁵And haply may forget.

CONTEXT

- Religious beliefs and attitudes
- Rossetti's belief in soul sleep
- Rossetti's romantic experiences

INTERPRETATION / ANALYSIS

When I am dead, my dearest,
Sing no sad songs for me;
Plant thou no roses at my head,
Nor shady cypress tree:
Be the green grass above me
With showers and dewdrops wet;
And if thou wilt, remember,
And if thou wilt, forget.

A partner poem to *Remember* in many ways, *Song's* speaker begins with direct address to her "dearest", implying perhaps a lover but, given Rossetti's own context, maybe her mother or sister, to whom she was very close indeed. The "when" implies that she has come to terms with the concept of death; it's simply an inevitability to be planned for

The speaker continues with a list of instructions that prevent commemoration – no singing (as at a funeral) and no planting by her grave. The "rose" carries the traditional connotations of love and romance – she is not to be overly mourned by her lover, but left naturally, with just the grass and rain – nature itself – to commemorate her. The "cypress tree" is an evergreen, and often planted as a memorial for that reason, so denying it adds to her desire that her lover not remember her.

The continuous negatives – no, not – throughout the poem may suggest that it doesn't matter whether the speaker is remembered on earth, which echoes Rossetti's religious belief in an afterlife. However, the concept of being simply forgotten would frighten most people – does Rossetti feel any doubt at her instructions?

The final couplet of the stanza gives the listener a choice – remember or forget. She uses "thou", indicating a very personal, intimate relationship, but the parallel structure of the two lines highlights this ambivalence - as though the speaker is indifferent to the decision.

There are also connotations here of the Victorian ideal woman – which extends to her being so grief-stricken at having to leave her lover that even in heaven, she is mourning their separation.

> **I shall not see the shadows,**
> **I shall not feel the rain;**
> **I shall not hear the nightingale**
> **Sing on, as if in pain:**
> **And dreaming through the twilight**
> **That doth not rise nor set,**
> **Haply I may remember,**
> **And haply may forget.**

Contrasting with the first stanza's insistence on "thou", this second stanza turns to the speaker's experience with her repeated "I shall not" Her trio of senses – "see, feel, hear" – is a further reminder that the earthly body will cease to have meaning. Here, the idea of the mourning spirit is also reversed – she will not feel any bodily sensations, and will not, perhaps, remember her lover either.

The "nightingale" is a frequent symbol in poetry, often imbued with desperate human emotion – Keats's *Ode to a Nightingale* for example. But Rossetti here recognises the imposition of human feelings onto the bird with her qualifying "as if" – she is aware that it's the human perception, not the nightingale's song, which is painful.

Instead of pain, the spirit will be "dreaming through the twilight" – both a reference to Rossetti's belief in "soul sleep" (See context at end of this guide) and a peaceful, calm image: death here is not painful anguish. Yet there's also a doubt present in the first three lines here – what will the after-life consist of; will she be able to see, feel or hear at all?

The final couplet is an inversion of the first stanza's, but also a rebuke to the lover who thinks their dead lover will mourn them – she, too, may remember or forget and neither is particularly emotive.

The final "haply" could be read either as "perhaps" – which implies that both is possible and she seems to feel nothing at either prospect – or "happily" – she's going to be happy and at peace in heaven, regardless of her earthly love.

STRUCTURE AND FORM

- **Elegy –** a poem of remembrance, commemorating the dead.
- **Repetition –** "no" and "not" are repeated frequently, emphasizing the lack of memory of the dead – ironic, perhaps, given the form of the elegy
- **Stanza structure –** the focus in stanza 1 on the lover, changed in the second stanza to the speaker
- **Iambic rhythm which falters –** primarily iambic, there are a few places where the rhythm changes, primarily on the word "remember", drawing attention to the poem's theme of memory
- **Balance –** the final couplet of each stanza, which inverts the expectations of traditional mourning (life your life)

CRITICAL INTERPRETATION

Therefore, the lines — "And if thou wilt, remember, / And if thou wilt, forget" — is not to ask her beloved to stop mourning her death in an attempt to embody "the Victorian view of female selflessness" (Landow). It instead invokes feelings of growing indifference towards her partner. Not only does the female voice in "Song" articulate indifference towards her supposed beloved, but also the woman seems to feel a sense of happiness in her inability to remember her beloved.

> And dreaming through the twilight
> That doth not rise nor set,
> Haply I may remember,
> And haply may forget.

The wordplay on "haply" can be interpreted as either "possibly" or a shortened version of the word "happily." This wordplay also helps destroy the feminine ideal as portrayed by Pre-Raphaelites such as Dante Rossetti by indicating that the woman perhaps realizes contentment and peace while without her beloved.

A Reversal of Roles in "Song [When I am Dead]"
Angela Kim '06, English/History of Art 151, Pre-Raphaelites, Aesthetes, and
Decadents, Brown University, 2004

CONNECTIONS

Love: Remember; No, Thank You, John; Echo
Memory: Remember; Shut Out; Echo
Death: Remember; Birthday; In The Round Tower
Earthly life and after-life: Echo; Birthday; Twice

¹I took my heart in my hand
(O my love, O my love),
I said: Let me fall or stand,
Let me live or die,
⁵But this once hear me speak--
(O my love, O my love) - -
Yet a woman's words are weak;
You should speak, not I.

You took my heart in your hand
¹⁰With a friendly smile,
With a critical eye you scanned,
Then set it down,
And said: It is still unripe,
Better wait awhile;
¹⁵Wait while the skylarks pipe,
Till the corn grows brown.

As you set it down it broke--
Broke, but I did not wince;
I smiled at the speech you spoke,
²⁰At your judgement that I heard:
But I have not often smiled
Since then, nor questioned since,
Nor cared for corn-flowers wild,
Nor sung with the singing bird.

²⁵I take my heart in my hand,
O my God, O my God,
My broken heart in my hand:
Thou hast seen, judge Thou.
My hope was written on sand,
³⁰O my God, O my God:
Now let thy judgement stand--
Yea, judge me now.

This contemned of a man,
This marred one heedless day,
³⁵This heart take Thou to scan
Both within and without:
Refine with fire its gold,
Purge thou its dross away--
Yea, hold it in Thy hold,
⁴⁰Whence none can pluck it out.

I take my heart in my hand--
I shall not die, but live--
Before Thy face I stand;
I, for Thou callest such:
⁴⁵All that I have I bring,
All that I am I give,
Smile Thou and I shall sing,
But shall not question much

CONTEXT:

Written in 1864, *Twice* was published in Rossetti's second collection **The Prince's Progress and Other Poems** – but at the beginning of the volume because of its focus on earthly, rather than heavenly, love. The poem tells the story of the female speaker offering her love to someone, but being rejected. When heartbroken, she offers her heart instead to God.

-   Rejection of marriage on religious grounds
-   Rossetti's religion
-   Attitude towards women's rights and independence

I took my heart in my hand
(O my love, O my love),
I said: Let me fall or stand,
Let me live or die,
But this once hear me speak--
(O my love, O my love)--
Yet a woman's words are weak;
You should speak, not I.

The aside "(O my love, O my love)" has the possessive exclamative of a lover but runs as a refrain through the first stanza yet as it is an aside, is it ever something that she truly feels is a part of her?

The challenging "let me fall or stand/let me live or die" is hyperbolic but expresses the intensity of first love; while "let" could seem a challenge to her love, it might also be a reckless throwing off of responsibility in her passionate moment.

She will only speak "but this once" Knowing that this is not the way gender relationships should work, declaring herself is risky, not only because expressing love exposes us to vulnerability like nothing else, but because the social conventions of the time frown on 'forward' women. This, she recognizes in the final lines of the stanza - "you should speak, not I" – as it is both his role in their relationship, and his turn once she has confessed her feelings.

You took my heart in your hand
With a friendly smile,
With a critical eye you scanned,
Then set it down,
And said: It is still unripe,
Better wait awhile;
Wait while the skylarks pipe,
Till the corn grows brown.

The first line is echoed but changed in this stanza, giving the choice – and action – to her lover. Is this a generous, loving gesture, handing herself over to him, symbolizing trust? Or is this, in a more religious interpretation, a loss of self-possession and self-control that she later regains through God?

In this patriarchal society, the lover takes authority and with his "friendly smile" and "critical eye" he is not cruel, but still does not reciprocate the gift she has given, instead destroying her ability to seek out earthly love. "Then set it down", with the short simple phrase on its own, emphasizes her sense of loss and disappointment. It's interestingly equivocal – is the lover older than the speaker, to suggest waiting a while? Or is there something more sexualized about this imagery – the idea of waiting for "ripeness", for the harvest of the corn. This might also imply that Victorian marriages are built on commerce and economics – the lover rejects her because the harvest is unripe, and therefore cannot be guaranteed profit. Yet when the harvest is ripe – and taken in – it becomes winter, and holds connotations of death and emptiness, unfilled potential. The harvest is precarious and can't always be relied upon.

The reference to skylarks could be influence by Percy Bysshe Shelley, whose poem "To A Skylark" (1820) positions a skylark as a source of divine inspiration: "In the light of thought/singing hymns unbidden." The skylark also sings in the daytime; is the lover suggesting waiting for a moment of joy before marrying?

> **As you set it down it broke--**
> **Broke, but I did not wince;**
> **I smiled at the speech you spoke,**
> **At your judgement that I heard:**
> **But I have not often smiled**
> **Since then, nor questioned since,**
> **Nor cared for corn-flowers wild,**
> **Nor sung with the singing bird.**

The direct address continues; is she explaining the past, and her later religious decision, to her lover? The repetition of "Broke / Broke" splits the repetition onto a new line to emphasize the disruption and pain of her broken heart, as well as the sudden nature of the damage caused. The dash causes a caesura, the moment the heart stops beating, followed by a trochee (*stressed/unstressed foot*) which disrupts the rhythm of the poem much as the broken heart would disrupt, creating the impression of a moment of breathlessness before the heart can resume. Yet she is also emotionally strong and does not "wince"; to show her pain to her potential lover would be humiliating and perhaps further embarrass or hurt her. The "but" indicates the connection; it is because of this incident that she is now miserable and trying to face the world alone. The repetitive "nor" indicates the negative possibilities of her life – the "cornflowers wild" and "singing bird" hold no value for her. They are joyful, a mocking reflection of the loneliness of her life at this point. She also though has "not questioned since" – she doesn't have the confidence to go back to her lover again (or has more pride than that!) and doesn't have the confidence to go elsewhere to look for earthly love. The possibility of joy – the skylark and harvest – in the previous stanza – has not come to pass.

> **I take my heart in my hand,**
> **O my God, O my God,**

> My broken heart in my hand:
>
> Thou hast seen, judge Thou.
>
> My hope was written on sand,
>
> O my God, O my God:
>
> Now let thy judgement stand--
>
> Yea, judge me now.

She regains her own authority – "**I** take my heart in my hand" – repeating the first line once more, but this time offering her love and devotion to someone else. Here the "O my love" is replaced with "O my God" – but no longer in an aside; is this an indication that the speaker has made her love for God more a part of herself than her love ever was? She uses "Thou" to address God, both a religious convention and a symbol of her respectful, loving relationship with Him. "My hope was written on sand" implies that she understands the fleeting, imperfect nature of her earthly love. It also has a Biblical connotation – "*Those who turn away from you will be written in the dust*" – which questions whether she is worthy of being accepted by God, having sought out the earthly love in preference to the heavenly. Yet it also suggests that this can be washed away by the incoming tide. The repetition of "O my God" becomes a plea, as she asks for his judgement. The speaker turns to God for the love she cannot find on earth.

> This contemned of a man,
>
> This marred one heedless day,
>
> This heart take Thou to scan
>
> Both within and without:
>
> Refine with fire its gold,
>
> Purge thou its dross away--
>
> Yea, hold it in Thy hold,
>
> Whence none can pluck it out.

Rossetti doesn't directly mention the heart until the third line - it is too painful, rejected and unworthy to be spoken of, but then she offers it to God despite it being damaged, "contemned" and "marred", although the phrase "of a man" implies the lesser contempt; is God willing to accept her where he was not?

"Refine with fire its gold/Purge thou its dross away" – holds several Biblical references. Purging with fire is a repeated image in the Bible, and the concept of a heart burning with the word of the lord is also repeatedly used in reference to hearing Christ speak. There is some language of sin and redemption - "purge", "refine". To refer to her heart as "dross" deeply rejects her previously earthly love as being little more than rubbish, to be cleansed. In the last two lines she completely gives herself over to God – "none can pluck it out", and she promises that nobody on earth will be able to remove her from God's love.

71

> **I take my heart in my hand--**
> **I shall not die, but live--**
> **Before Thy face I stand;**
> **I, for Thou callest such:**
> **All that I have I bring,**
> **All that I am I give,**
> **Smile Thou and I shall sing,**
> **But shall not question much.**

Here, the first line is the same as the first stanza, implying the resolution to her experiences and decision. "I shall not die but live" echoes the Christian belief that eternal life with God requires dying on earth; for Rossetti, giving up her earthly loves in order to be worth of her divine love.

The middle two lines – "All that I have I bring/All that I am I give" echoes the liturgy of commitment (see *below*) from the marriage ceremony, during the exchanging of rings: this is a symbolic marriage to God, her dedicating herself to Him and Him alone. She writes of being "callest", as though she is suggesting loving God is a calling – a vocation, perhaps, similar to the intensity felt by a nun. She implies at the end that her happiness is fully in God's love – "Smile Thou and I shall sing" – bringing to mind the hymns of a church congregation, singing to God. However, there is a slight note of doubt at the end: when she promises she "shall not question **much**" is she being playful and teasing, or is there a rueful acceptance that in fact she cannot help but continue to have occasional doubts, that she will try to suppress?

- **Frequent repetition** including the slight shifting of the refrain - *Oh my love/Oh my god* and */You take/took my heart* – to emphasizes the shifting spiritual and emotional changes of the speaker.
- **Rhyme scheme** is usually abacdbdc but in stanza 4 it becomes abacabac – the middle line being a repetition of "O my God, O my God", demonstrating the determination to present herself to God.
- **Meter** (the stressed syllables) falls on key words to reflect the determination of the speaker, e.g stanza 1 "love, hand, let, fall, stand." Reading aloud is essential to hear this.
- **A change** in the middle of the poem, when the speaker begins to address God rather than her earthly lover
- A **dramatic monologue** spoken to an unseen listener, this also has elements of **narrative** and **lyric**.

CRITICAL INTERPRETATIONS

"Twice" operates at a level of cultural criticism different from that of "Light Love" and "An Apple-Gathering." The attack implicit in its six brief stanzas is upon the powerlessness of women in a rigid patriarchal society. The man's words are spoken with absolute and final authority. But the poem subverts the premises underlying that authority by appealing to a higher one who can be imaginatively idealized as a worthy judge and lover. He can be constructed in the image of a genuinely sympathetic and receptive — that is, an ironically non-sexist — being. Along with the sanctions of love in approved social forms and contexts, the speaker here indignantly and impatiently renounces the natural world, and, now penitent for her presumptuous erotic quest, she approaches God

She thus acknowledges the uncertainty of *eros*, but also, aware that her quest for earthly love was misguided, she acknowledges her need to be chastened and "purged" in order to become worthy of Gods superior love. Alienated from the arbitrary and insensitive values of her patriarchal society, the speaker in "Twice," like the persona of "A Birthday" and the lover in "Dream-Love," finds herself to be an alien in the natural world as well. Like Yeats's persona in "Sailing to Byzantium," she perceives her heart, finally, as an artifact that

The liturgy of commitment:

I give you this ring
as a sign of our marriage.
With my body I honour you,
all that I am I give to you,
and all that I have I share with you,
within the love of God,

can be "refined" and perfected only when it is "once out of nature," projected wholly either into the world of art or the realm of the ideal. Such is the case in all of Christina Rossetti's poems whose focus is not on the possibility of fulfilling earthly love, or upon betrayal in love, but rather upon the apparently inevitable culmination of all compulsive amatory passions — renunciation.

Love and Betrayal in the Poetry of Christina Rossetti
Anthony H. Harrison, Professor of English, North Carolina State University

CONNECTIONS

Love – No, Thank You John; Winter: My Secret; Maude Clare; Song (When I am Dead)

Imagery of nature: A Birthday; Maude Clare; Echo

Religion: Shut Out; Soeur Louise; Good Friday; Song (When I am Dead)

Conflict of Earth and Heaven: Remember; Song (When I am Dead)

UPHILL

¹Does the road wind up-hill all the way?
Yes, to the very end.
Will the day's journey take the whole long day?
From morn to night, my friend.

⁵But is there for the night a resting-place?
A roof for when the slow dark hours begin.
May not the darkness hide it from my face?
You cannot miss that inn.

Shall I meet other wayfarers at night?
¹⁰Those who have gone before.
Then must I knock, or call when just in sight?
They will not keep you standing at that door.

Shall I find comfort, travel-sore and weak?
Of labour you shall find the sum.
¹⁵Will there be beds for me and all who seek?
Yea, beds for all who come.

CONTEXT

Composed in 1858, and published in Macmillan's Magazine in 1861, *Uphill* was included in the devotional section of *Goblin Market and Other Poems*. The magazine was one of the most significant literary journals of the period – incredibly popular, and Rossetti's publication was significant in bringing her to the attention of a wider audience.

INTERPRETATION / ANALYSIS

Does the road wind up-hill all the way?
Yes, to the very end.
Will the day's journey take the whole long day?
From morn to night, my friend.

This poem, from the religious section of *Goblin Market and Other Poems*, starts with the question / answer format that runs through the whole piece – it expresses doubt, and the speaker's need to know what will happen to them in the afterlife. While this can be read as a very simple exchange between two characters, it seems more likely given its placement in the collection, that this is a conversation between a persona and a religious figure – perhaps Jesus or God themselves, or maybe a vicar or similar representative.

Symbolizing life as a journey is a fairly well-worn path (excusing the pun!). Rossetti would have been familiar with *Pilgrim's Progress* by John Bunyan, where the Christian has to plough their way through several cities and trials on their way to heaven, the Celestial City. The day, or life, is "long", from "morn to night" or birth until death. The "up-hill" nature of the journey implies that life continues to be difficult, and that trials must be experienced and overcome in order to reach the end. The winding nature of the road also shows the length of it; there is no direct way through, and everyone must find their own way. Ending the stanza with "my friend", though, makes this journey appear as though there is a welcome waiting at the end, when the questioner reaches heaven.

> **But is there for the night a resting-place?**
> **A roof for when the slow dark hours begin.**
> **May not the darkness hide it from my face?**
> **You cannot miss that inn.**

When the night – or death – arrives, the questioner longs for a resting place. The night, death itself, is described in difficult terms, "slow dark", repeating "darkness", something from which the questioner needs solace and shelter. There is a tone of doubt in the whole poem, not only through the nature of the question and answer, but the worry that they might miss the inn ("May not the darkness hide it from my face?"). But the reassuring response is always unequivocal, a short firm statement: "you cannot miss that inn".

The sense of doubt here is seen in several of Rossetti's religious poems – in *Good Friday* in particular, the speaker is worried that because she doubts, her faith will not be enough to see her through. However here in the question and answer we have doubt and reassurance – the responder is gentle and kind with the questioner's lack of faith.

> **Shall I meet other wayfarers at night?**
> **Those who have gone before.**
> **Then must I knock, or call when just in sight?**
> **They will not keep you standing at that door.**

This might be a reference to a particular Bible verse:

Here I am! I stand at the door and knock. If anyone hears my voice and opens the door, I will come in and eat with them and they with me. *Revelation 3:20*

The imagery of the door is also familiar in Rossetti's collection. In *Shut Out*, the garden is firmly closed to the speaker and in *Winter: My Secret* the speaker "cannot ope to everyone who taps", and is discerning as to who she opens up to. However when it comes to imagery of heaven, the door is more often being opened to allow the newly-dead to enter – a more welcoming, promising view of the afterlife. The reference to "wayfarers" could be a reference to Rossetti's own loved ones (see the contextual information) but it may also be more generic and refer to anyone who has previously died, and therefore found their own way along the road. The welcoming tone is again created by the modal "will not keep you standing at that door", the implication being that she will be instead welcomed in. The questioner also will not need to "knock" or "call" – which could be a suggestion that God is forgiving of all regardless of their beliefs: again, a reassurance against doubt or loss of faith.

> **Shall I find comfort, travel-sore and weak?**
> **Of labour you shall find the sum.**
> **Will there be beds for me and all who seek?**
> **Yea, beds for all who come.**

Again this might be a close bible reference:

My Father's house has plenty of room; if that were not so, would I have told you that I am going there to prepare a place for you? And if I go and prepare a place for you, I will come back and take you to be with me that you also may be where I am. *John 14:2-3*

Yet despite the reassurance, this safe haven doesn't come for free but "of labour you shall find the sum" – not *quite* welcoming; heaven here is certainly a reward for earthly endeavour, which reflects Rossetti's branch of Christianity. Ending the stanza with "yea, beds for all who come", echoes the opening "yes, to the very end", but with the change to "yea" sounds more archaic and highlights the religious nature of the poem. Ending with this short, declarative sentence implies the end to the questions, that even if doubt remains, reassurance has been given.

STRUCTURE AND FORM

- **Primarily iambic rhythm** to create a walking pace and tone, and suggest the regularity of the walking through life that must happen. This works together with the stanza structure.
- **Quatrains, with an abab rhyme scheme** – the regularity here could suggest the monotony and laborious nature of the journey through life towards salvation. Rossetti did believe that life needed moral works in order to earn a place in heaven – the "labour" of the poem – and so often expressed life's difficulties as testing religious conviction
- **Question/answer structure** – highlights the nature of religious doubt, and the reassuring nature of the conversation. Is the answerer a version of God or Jesus, a priest or vicar, or is it someone else who's giving the doubtful faith? Whichever is the case, the conflict between doubt and faith – and whether doubt is crippling, something to be lived with, or something to be overcome, is

a concern of the poem. Questioning here is accepted, even encouraged – because there will always be reassurance given.

CRITICAL INTERPRETATIONS

In this passage, the door spoken of refers to the acceptance of Jesus in the human heart. In Uphill, the one knocking at the door is not Jesus but the traveller. However, the responsibility for creating an environment in which the door is ready to be opened lies with the individual - it is the speaker's choice whether or not to persevere on the journey in time to reach the inn.

(http://crossref-it.info/textguide/christina-rossetti-selected-poems/28/1885)

CONNECTIONS

Imagery of the door – Remember, Shut Out, Winter: My Secret
Religion and the afterlife: Shut Out; Soeur Louise; Good Friday; Song (When I am Dead); Remember
Soul-sleep: Remember, Song

¹I tell my secret? No indeed, not I:
Perhaps some day, who knows?
But not today; it froze, and blows, and snows,
And you're too curious: fie!
⁵You want to hear it? well:
Only, my secret's mine, and I won't tell. –

Or, after all, perhaps there's none:
Suppose there is no secret after all,
But only just my fun.
¹⁰Today's a nipping day, a biting day;
In which one wants a shawl,
A veil, a cloak, and other wraps:
I cannot ope to everyone who taps,
And let the draughts come whistling thro' my hall;
¹⁵Come bounding and surrounding me,
Come buffeting, astounding me,
Nipping and clipping thro' my wraps and all.
I wear my mask for warmth: who ever shows
His nose to Russian snows
²⁰To be pecked at by every wind that blows?
You would not peck? I thank you for good will,
Believe, but leave the truth untested still.

Spring's an expansive time: yet I don't trust
March with its peck of dust,
²⁵Nor April with its rainbow-crowned brief showers,
Nor even May, whose flowers
One frost may wither thro' the sunless hours.

Perhaps some languid summer day,
When drowsy birds sing less and less,
³⁰And golden fruit is ripening to excess,
If there's not too much sun nor too much cloud,
And the warm wind is neither still nor loud,
Perhaps my secret I may say,
Or you may guess.

CONTEXT:

First published in <u>Goblin Market and Other Poems</u> – a non-devotional collection published in 1862 – Rossetti's first public collection. Its draft title was Nonsense, according to her brother William Michael Rossetti. Is this perhaps an indication that there is no secret at all? Is the poem more about the art of secret-keeping and illusion?

INTERPRETATION / ANALYSIS

The title itself has connotations of something cold, depressed – a refusal to tell. The colon implies a relationship; "My secret" is an elaboration on winter – pauses inherently make us wait for what follows, and here Rossetti makes the reader wait for the secret to be revealed.

> ¹I tell my secret? No indeed, not I:
> Perhaps some day, who knows?
> But not today; it froze, and blows, and snows,
> And you're too curious: fie!
> ⁵You want to hear it? well:
> Only, my secret's mine, and I won't tell. –

This is another narrative poem, like *No Thank You, John*, speaking to an unseen listener who becomes more insistent as the poem continues. There's a playful and questioning tone established at the beginning through the repeated rhetorical questions. Her intention is always clear from the outset – she will **not** tell her secret, yet we, like the listener, continue to read, certain that she will, eventually, give up her information to us.

"Winter" has connotations of cold, harsh distance, unloving. It's a perfect time for concealment, and trial. The snow is potentially destructive – it will come and freeze her to death if she'll let it so she needs to protect herself against it. Yet the syndetic rhyming of "froze, and blows, and snows" is also playful, elongating the line and creating a sing-song tone, teasing her listener. The caesura at "but not today;" is another hint

When she accuses the listener – "you're too curious, fie!" – (*fie being an interjection like hah! expressing scorn*), is it defensive or sarcastic – is the listener to intent on her giving up her secret? The theme of curiosity is frequent – in *Goblin Market*, it's Laura's downfall, and it links to religious undertones, the curiosity of mankind losing them the Garden of Eden. Is this an attempt at a sexual encounter? There's certainly some suggestions in later stanzas regarding the woman's clothing.

Rossetti's speaker uses repetitive personal pronouns - "my"/ "mine"/ "I" – to indicate her possessive nature over her secret; she will not share with anyone, and this also creates a sense or personal identity; the secret is hers and hers alone.

Or, after all, perhaps there's none:
Suppose there is no secret after all,
But only just my fun.
¹⁰Today's a nipping day, a biting day;
In which one wants a shawl,
A veil, a cloak, and other wraps:
I cannot ope to everyone who taps,
And let the draughts come whistling thro' my hall;
¹⁵Come bounding and surrounding me,
Come buffeting, astounding me,
Nipping and clipping thro' my wraps and all.
I wear my mask for warmth: who ever shows
His nose to Russian snows
²⁰To be pecked at by every wind that blows?
You would not peck? I thank you for good will,
Believe, but leave the truth untested still.

The speaker introduces another layer of intrigue – perhaps there's no secret at all – yet still we stay and hope she'll give it up. The "fun" highlights the teasing tone of the poem, coming at the end of an unusually short line. Here, the speaker seems more under attack and the language of cold, the semantic field, gets more aggressive, "nipping" and "biting", which also have some more rough sexual connotations, if you interpret this poem as being about women's sexual independence. The clothing lends weight to the interpretation of the speaker as female (remembering of course that these personas in this poem, *No, Thank You John,* and others, aren't necessarily a version of Rossetti herself) as she wears a "veil" and a "shawl" but more importantly has a hiding function; she can wrap herself in multiple layers and hide herself and her secret away. The "mask for warmth" is comforting to her – sometimes having a secret makes you feel special, loved, comforted and special. The clothing is almost theatrical, with that idea of a mask – why does she shroud herself in so much of it?

Rossetti's metaphor of the door appears again ("I cannot ope to everyone who taps") adding to the speaker's sense of vulnerability as once the secret is out it is gone, and may as well be everyone's. It will cease to give her warmth and protection – she'll be vulnerable to "draughts" and "Russian snows". The metaphor of the door is found frequently in Rossetti's poetry, often as a door to heaven although that doesn't seem to work here – there are few other suggestions this is a religious poem – but the door is usually being opened rather than being held fast shut. In *Shut Out*, however, the door is held shut and both poems have an element of warning against sexuality – in *Shut Out*, the door to Eden is closed after Eve's curiosity and here the speaker must keep the door shut or will risk being open to everyone – desire, once admitted, is all-consuming and potentially destroying.

The gerunds in the second half – bounding, surrounding, buffeting, astounding, nipping, clipping, - create a startling sense of immediacy, the vibrant urgency of the present tense. Is the listener becoming more insistent? It sounds here like the speaker is becoming more defensive. The description of being "pecked at by every wind" is harsh and cold, like the title, but also becomes more metaphoric with the rhetorical question "You would not peck?" which again could have sexual, or aggressive, undertones. There's clearly a lack of trust here too. The rhetorical question seems to be an echo of the listener's unheard response to her concerns; she thanks but insists she still does not trust his (?) good intentions and will not put them to the test. This poem could be a warning to women – men seem trustworthy, but is it worth allowing them the opportunity?

Eating often features as a form of attack or punishment; here through pecking, nipping, biting (contrast with *Goblin Market*?) However, are these verbs also indications of sexual playfulness?

> **Spring's an expansive time: yet I don't trust**
> **March with its peck of dust,**
> **25Nor April with its rainbow-crowned brief showers,**
> **Nor even May, whose flowers**
> **One frost may wither thro' the sunless hours.**

The relatively short stanza here contrasts with the previous longer one, explaining the difficulties to her listener. Here instead she explains her lack of trust through the symbolism of changing seasons, which are not as reliable as winter. Spring is "expansive" which has connotations of bravado or arrogance -it literally means "frank and communicative", the complete opposite of the wintry secret. Traditionally spring's also associated with birth and renewal, but she presents it as fleeting and untrustworthy. The spring flowers and brief showers may be symbolic of the revealed secret, quickly destroyed when exposed to the elements or, in the sectet's case, exposed to those who know it. The seasons are changeable and unpredictable. March has the "peck of dust" ("peck" now being a noun, a flurry of unexpected snow). April has "brief" showers and the rainbow-crown subverts the usual optimism of the rainbow into something more duplicitous. May is still susceptible to flower-killing frosts. Only winter remains reliable,

82

solid, and expected – solitude and keeping her secret, despite the cold, is the only option that is favourable. Maybe this symbolizes Rossetti's attitudes to love, desire and trust: they aren't worth the risk, when solitude and religious feeling are reliable and predictable and, with the clothing of the second stanza, can be warm too.

> **Perhaps some languid summer day,**
> **When drowsy birds sing less and less,**
> **[30]And golden fruit is ripening to excess,**
> **If there's not too much sun nor too much cloud,**
> **And the warm wind is neither still nor loud,**
> **Perhaps my secret I may say,**
> **Or you may guess.**

The conditional "perhaps" brings back the teasing playful tone, with the tantalizing prospect of the possibility that she will tell her secret. Summer is the opposite to the harshness of winter; languid, drowsy, but excessive – and therefore also not to be trusted. The sun, cloud and wind are too unreliable to be trusted with her secrets. Perhaps only when the listener has lost interest in the secret will she reveal it.

The birds are another frequent image, used here to bring to mind the sleepy heat of summer. In other poems, they also symbolize the depth of feeling of the speaker. The reference to eating is here again, with the "golden fruit" but it ripens "to excess", becoming spoiled and uneatable, This could suggest that her secret, once shared, will be ruined. In a reading of the poem on desire, it also suggests that the "ripeness" of woman is spoiled once she gives into men's desire.

The final short line "Or you may guess" is both tantalizing and infuriating. We knew from the beginning that she wouldn't tell us, but the invitation to guess remains (as if she would tell us if we were right!) The lack of closure is also important; Rossetti's poems often unsettle because of their internal contradictions and challenges – here she refuses to suggest a resolution. The open-ended, ambiguous nature of language itself suggests that there is a potential for a new, disorienting, world view - often the reader is delivered back to their world and the uncertainties of the new refuted. With a lack of closure, attention is drawn to the distance between the conventional and the new.

STRUCTURE AND FORM

- **Dramatic monologue** – spoken to an unseen listener and putting the reader in their position: we want to know the secret as much as they do, and become just as infuriated at her refusal to tell.
- **Changing line lengths** – the short lines in particular draw attention to the teasing tone, e.g. the last line, and "but only just my fun".

83

- **Iambic rhythm** creates a sense of natural speech but the irregularity of the line length means that this sounds more natural. The irregularity (Rossetti uses a combination of iambic pentameter, tetrameter and trimeter) also makes it difficult to predict, like the speaker herself.
- **Repeated motifs** of cold, and of attacking movements
- **Rhyme** is in couplets and triplets, increasing pace as she answers more vehemently and remains unpredictable. The second stanza is loaded with simple monosyllabic masculine rhymes; listeners try to identify the scheme, what should come next -but they're unable to follow and keep up, noting only once it has been revealed, and never able to predict.

CRITICAL INTERPRETATIONS

Given that Rossetti doesn't really do excellent titles (often) her choice is interesting; it implies it's something intriguing, to be explored – developing the theme of curiosity immediately. Dinah Roe calls the entire poem a "verbal striptease": if she were to "ope" herself to all it would potentially be very dangerous. She reveals gradually, teasingly – and then uses the final provocative "guess".

Dinah Roe

"more importantly, the speaker, the owner of the "mask" asserts her right to speak her own thoughts."

Dolores Rosenblum's 'Christina Rossetti: the Poetry of Endurance" (1988):

"Throughout the poem, the existence of the secret remains ambiguous and its content uncertain. Indeed, in the manuscript version of the poem, an empty space serves as ta placeholder for the very word "secret": "Only my <   > mine…." Even while the poem holds forth on the secret, it therefore withholds it as well."

Cambridge Companion to Victorian Poetry:

"Closure, however, very often embodies a literal resignation of the rebelliousness of language, themes, and characterization within the works, a giving over of the potential evoked in the poems for destabilizing the conventional world (of language, social expectations, literary conventions) in which the poems are usually set."

Anthony H. Harrison, Professor of English, North Carolina State University

"Behind this playfulness, however, is an intriguing study in the manipulation of power. For the speaker denies entry to the reader and instead metaphorically wraps herself in protective clothing which will keep others out. Her privacy is not to be intruded upon and she consequently leaves the reader guessing at her knowledge….This therefore becomes an intriguing poem about what is not said, where the speaker skillfully withholds power and control. The game is hers and she will only 'tell' when and if she chooses.

In poems such as these, then, Rossetti's speakers demonstrate both an awareness of, and resistance to, those social and political expectations which define acceptable roles for women and which potentially leave them powerless. While poems such as 'From the Antique' and 'In an Artist's Studio' emphasize the ways in which women might be trapped by convention, other poems such as 'Maude Clare', 'No, Thank You, John', and 'Winter: My Secret' reveal a much more complex negotiation of power which enables the women to achieve agency, equality and self-sufficiency. As such, Rossetti's poems make an intriguing contribution to those crucial debates around the Woman Question and gender relations which were central to the second half of the nineteenth century and beyond.

Simon Avery, British Library

CONNECTIONS

Women's difficulties in society – No, Thank You, John; Maude Clare)
Curiosity and its downfalls: No, Thank You, John; Goblin Market;
Sexual desire: Shut Out; Soeur Louise;
Imagery: Birds (Birthday; Maude Clare; Song When I am Dead) and doors (Shut Out; Echo; Uphill)

The question will be made up of two parts – the first sentence will be a specific theme and poem. The second will remain the same, and remind you to analyze language, form and structure and to compare Rossetti's poem with the rest of the collection.

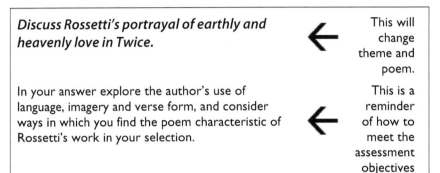

Discuss Rossetti's portrayal of earthly and heavenly love in Twice.

This will change theme and poem.

In your answer explore the author's use of language, imagery and verse form, and consider ways in which you find the poem characteristic of Rossetti's work in your selection.

This is a reminder of how to meet the assessment objectives

Possible starting phrases for the question:

Discuss Rossetti's portrayal of:

- religious doubt
- the afterlife
- male and female relationships
- women's independence
- women's authority
- masculinity
- femininity
- sisterhood
- secrecy
- the overt and covert
- exclusion

- nature
- painful love
- joyful love
- difficulties in love
- relationships of art and poetry
- marriage
- faith
- desire
- destructive tendencies
- nature
- Commerce and exchange

At A-Level, you're being asked to compare these poems with a pre-1900 drama text. Because there are so many choices, there is a wide range of questions available – which can be of-putting because it seems overwhelming – but it's not really!

The question will look like this:

A list of the text choices. Remember – you have studied one from each list!

Reminder of your timings

Section 2 – Drama and Poetry pre-1900

Answer **one** question from this section. You should spend about 1 hour and 15 minutes on this section.

In your answer, you should refer to one drama text and one poetry text from the following lists:

Drama	Poetry
Christopher Marlowe: *Edward II* John Webster: *The Duchess of Malfi* Oliver Goldsmith: *She Stoops to Conquer* Henrik Ibsen: *A Doll's House* Oscar Wilde: *An Ideal Husband*	Geoffrey Chaucer: *The Merchant's Prologue and Tale* John Milton: *Paradise Lost Books 9 & 10* Samuel Taylor Coleridge: *Selected Poems* Alfred, Lord Tennyson: *Maud* Christina Rossetti: *Selected Poems*

Six question choices – see next page for how to choose!

Endings are always, in some sense, artificial.'
In the light of this view, consider ways in which writers conclude their work.

'What can male writers know or understand about women?'
In the light of this view, consider ways in which writers present women.

'Arrogance is the most monstrous of faults.'
In the light of this view, consider ways in which writers portray arrogance.

'It is rarely good for us to get what we want.'
In the light of this view, consider ways in which writers portray appetites and desires, and their consequences.

'Wrongdoing and villainy can provoke both admiration and disgust at the same time.'
In the light of this view, consider ways in which writers present wrongdoing and villainy.

'Seduction is most effectively accomplished through flattery.'
In the light of this view, consider ways in which writers represent seduction.

Although it can seem tricky with so many options, start by removing the questions you **don't want to answer** – put a cross by them.

87

1. For example, if studying Rossetti then perhaps the "male writers" question isn't the best choice.
2. With short poems like hers, also consider crossing out the "Endings" question (more suitable to longer poetry perhaps). So we're down to four.
3. Does she explore villainy? Not a lot. And let's also take "arrogance" off the list as it limits which poems we can write about.
4. So now, we're down to "it's rarely good to get what we want" and "seduction is accomplished through flattery." Well, I know which I would choose!

Endings are always, in some sense, artificial.'
In the light of this view, consider ways in which writers conclude their work.

'What can male writers know or understand about women?'
In the light of this view, consider ways in which writers present women.

'Arrogance is the most monstrous of faults.'
In the light of this view, consider ways in which writers portray arrogance.

'It is rarely good for us to get what we want.'
In the light of this view, consider ways in which writers portray appetites and desires, and their consequences.

'Wrongdoing and villainy can provoke both admiration and disgust at the same time.'
In the light of this view, consider ways in which writers present wrongdoing and villainy.

'Seduction is most effectively accomplished through flattery.'
In the light of this view, consider ways in which writers represent seduction.

Of course, you have to also consider your second text and there's no reason why you *couldn't* write about, say, the male writers understanding women – John Webster in The Duchess of Malfi, for example, or Ibsen's portrayal of Nora in A Doll's House, and then make a reasonable argument that their portrayal is just as believable, rich and complex as Rossetti's – imagination knows no gender.

BUT you'll find that some questions you dislike immediately – so cross them out. **There are no additional marks for choosing something you find hard!**

And you might find that some questions you like immediately.

With those, it's always worth making a quick bullet-point plan just to be sure that you can write enough.

HOW TO ADDRESS THE ASSESSMENT OBJECTIVES IN AN ESSAY

This differs hugely between AS and A Level.

At AS Level

Because your dominant assessment objective is AO2, followed by AO1 and AO4, you need to focus primarily on language, form and structure. Each paragraph needs t explore the **methods** that Rossetti uses in this poem and then "fan out" into several other poems, with context interwoven. A sample plan might look like this:

Door
symbolism -
Link: Shut Out
Context -

Beauty of language -
sunlight, bright etc.
Glorying in heaven
Link: Birthday (halcyon rainbow)

Context - Religious beliefs

Discuss Rossetti's presentation of the afterlife in Echo

Repeated
imperative
"come";
emphasis on
longing, desire.
Link: Song When

Imagery of death - thirsting
longing, pulse, breath
Link: Remember
Context: family deaths

This **begins** with AO2, then links a poem that has a similar idea or technique, and then brings in contextual understanding, but integrates it with the theme of the question.

At A Level

As AO3 is the dominant objectives, a different balance has to be struck- you have to create a strong impression of contextual understanding *without* sounding like a History essay! You need to avoid it being simply a comparison of, say, women's lives in different eras, or different politics in Rossetti and Ibsen.

Again, remember that OCR is a holistic marker – they want a good essay *shaded* in the direction of context. Including a strong contextual comparison in the introduction is useful. Equally useful is starting paragraphs with context, to keep you on track.

Remember that **form** is also contextual – how the writers approach themes differently **because** they have chosen poetry or drama is important.

89

"Context" basically means; how is a poet affected by their life, time and circumstance, and how is our reading of their work affected by **our** life, time and circumstances.

There is a *lot* of information about Rossetti's life and biography which I find fascinating! But for this guide, I have focused on what I think is most useful in helping you to understand and interpret the poems. If you're interested in knowing more, I highly recommend Jan Marsh's biography. What you definitely **don't** want to be doing is dumping information about Rossetti's family at the end of a paragraph. Everything you comment on about Rossetti's context needs to be used to help explore the meaning of the poem you're writing about.

CONTEXT FOR A-LEVEL

Although the basic definition is the same, there is a stronger weighting for context, so you can consider in the difference between the poetry and drama texts:

- Reference to other related texts (e.g. comparing Rossetti's lack of political poetry with Elizabeth Barrett Browning, who was well-known for her more politicized works).
- Production details – which collections poems were originally from, and when they were published.
- Critical response – contemporary and since.
- Political.
- Social.
- Religious including morality norms of society at the time.
- Environmental (how their own personal circumstances including family history contributed to their view of the world).
- Attitude to relationships and sexuality – the writer's and society's more widely.
- The dominance of patriarchal or feminist thinking (particularly when comparing to some of the plays).
- Genre expectations – for the plays, this might be comedy, tragedy, realism etc. For Rossetti, consider Goblin Market's use of the oral tradition, for example, or Maude Clare as a ballad. Remember, too, the expectations of *poetry* contrasted with *drama* – although AO2 Form isn't assessed individuality, it contributes enormously to the context of the piece.
- Literary context – using common interpretations of symbols or iconography.
- How challenging or supportive the writers are of contemporary social norms and ideals.

- Different critical responses – both named, individual critics and schools of thought (Marxism, Feminism, Freudian)

FAMILY HISTORY

Christina Rossetti was born in 1830, meaning she was 7 when Queen Victoria ascended the throne at 18. Rossetti's family was very intellectual and well-educated. It's a common myth that Victorian women weren't educated – while Rossetti didn't go to school, she was mostly home-educated, read Keats, Scott and Dante (her father was Italian, so she also read other Italian writers). Her home was filled with scholars and artists, so she had a lot of highly intellectual influences. Her uncle, incidentally, was John Polidori, Lord Byron's physician, who wrote *The Vampyre* on a holiday in Switzerland with Byron and the Shelleys, during which Mary Shelley also wrote *Frankenstein*. (Ok, so that bit doesn't help interpret the poetry, but isn't it a cool fact?!)

There was a lot of illness in her family – in particular her father suffered bronchitis, probably TB, and impending blindness, which also caused depression. Because he was the main income-earner, this also caused tremendous financial difficulties, meaning her mother began teaching and her sister Maria began working as a live-in governess. As her other siblings were away working or in education, she became increasingly isolated and lonely. At 14, she was diagnosed with religious mania after a nervous breakdown.

Christina's sister Maria later joined a religious order as a nun.

One brother was Dante Gabriel Rossetti, who was a painter and one of the founders of the Pre-Raphaelite movement, looking back to art styles of the Italian Renaissance, and using ideas from the medieval period to reinterpret the modern. Among some of their most famous paintings are the version of Ophelia by John Millais, using the model Lizzie Siddall who later married Dante Gabriel, and Lady Lilith, by Dante Gabriel. Dante and Lizzie were both drug addicts, and Lizzie died of an overdose – Dante never really got over

Lady Lilith. by Dante Gabriel Rossetti

Goblin Market

her death.

Christina never married (see below) but had a very close relationship with her siblings and mother, and remained living with her mother for most of her life.

91

She became very ill herself in later life, suffering from Graves disease for nearly twenty years, a serious thyroid illness which in Rossetti contributed to a diminished physical appearance which made her more reclusive than ever. She also developed breast cancer, which killed her. She did in 1894, and is buried in Highgate Cemetery in London with her parents.

How to apply this:

Poems of death and loss could be linked with Rossetti's early experiences of family illness and death. Her relationship with her sister was extremely close, and could be connected with the sisters of *Goblin Market* while *Soeur Louise* might also have been influenced by her desire to understand what her sister is giving up by becoming a nun.

Ophelia, by John Millais

MARRIAGE AND RELATIONSHIPS

Christina has several relationships which progressed towards engagement. Fin her late teens, she became engaged to James Collinson, a painter in the Pre-Raphaelite movement with Dante. She broke the engagement off when he became a Catholic in 1850. Later on, Charles Cayley (a noted linguist) proposed, but she rejected him because he couldn't share her Anglican faith, which was essential to her. Her brother William said "Although she would not be his wife no woman ever loved a man more deeply or constantly." They remained very close friends until his death, when he left her all his manuscripts. Several of her collections are dedicated to the children of either her brother William or Charles Cayley, and it seems that Rossetti had a continual sadness at her own childlessness, but found comfort with these children.
She was also proposed to by John Brett, but refused him as well.

How to apply this:

Some of her poems express ideas about romantic love which are both beautiful, joyful, and painful. Some also express the difficulty of choosing between earthly romantic love and heavenly love, which she evidently had to do at least twice and led her to great soul-searching and heartbreak.

BELIEFS ABOUT WOMEN'S ROLE IN SOCIETY

Christina and Maria both volunteered at the St Mary Magdalene penitentiary (not a prison, despite the name). It was a "house of charity", a refuge for former prostitute and 'fallen women'. Many of Rossetti's poems express distaste for the double standards of the time, particularly regarding sexual morality. She appears to dislike the duality of women, either maid or temptress, and is often angry that the men who "get" women into trouble bear no responsibility for their part in ruining women's lives. She also has a relatively progressive view that a mistake or sexual misdemeanor should not condemn a woman for the rest of her life.

Women's rights changed enormously during the Victorian era, but for the majority of the time in which Rossetti was writing, married women couldn't own property, and

In the 1870s, Rossetti was asked to support a campaign to give women the vote. Rossetti refused, writing:

> Does it not appear as if the Bible was based upon an understood unalterable distinction between men and women, their position, duties, privileges? On the other hand if female rights are sure to be overborne for lack of female voting influence, then I confess I feel disposed to shoot ahead of my instructresses, and to assert that female M.P's are only right and reasonable. Also I take exceptions at the exclusion of married women from the suffrage, — for who so apt as Mothers — all previous arguments allowed for the moment — to protect the interests of themselves and of their offspring? I do think if anything ever does sweep away the barrier of sex, and make the female not a giantess or a heroine but at once and full grown a hero and giant, it is that mighty maternal love which makes little birds and little beasts as well as little women matches for very big adversaries.

To a modern reader. it can appear that this might negate any feminist interpretation of her poetry – how can she be a feminist if she's against women voting? But her addition suggests that Rossetti, while not a modern feminist, does see women as equal in many ways – but emphatically very different, with different responsibilities. It wasn't an uncommon Victorian view; while some people did want the stereotypical view we often now have of Victorian women, the angel in the house, weak passive and docile, many

93

saw women as essential leaders of Britain's domestic, moral and spiritual life, while men were suited to the political – both important, but different. In a world where ideas about women's rights were changing dramatically, her thinking on the matter is extremely complex and detailed – and changes over time.

How to apply this:

Rossetti frequently explores women's roles, in particular the double standards regarding men and women. She also considers women's own authority and power – where they have the right to say no, to hide themselves, to control their own lives. Even when this isn't necessarily the *sole* point of the poem, Rossetti's writing from a female perspective often means it's present – in *Song*, for example, she writes the female response to a clichéd view of the silent dead woman grieving for her loved one from the afterlife. In *Winter: My Secret*, the speaker claims authority to tell what she likes, and in *From the Antique* she decries the poverty of a woman's rights and roles.

POLITICS

Although Christina didn't get particularly involved in politics, she was opposed to slavery in the American south, and wrote about topics including the cruel practices of animal experimentation, and the use of children in prostitution.

How to apply this:

Most of the collection doesn't have a directly political leaning, however, there is scope for a comment on the lack of politics considering the huge changes occurring in the Victorian era, and the contrasting discussion in other works. Many writers of all genres engaged with these issues; Rossetti lived in a highly academic community in London, yet remained isolated and did not put much of this public conversation into her poetry, preferring to use it for personal exploration. The exception is, of course, her portrayal of women as discussed above.

RELIGION

Christina was an Anglican, specifically a Tractarian – a branch of Christianity that emphasizes ritual and ceremony in worship. They particularly enjoyed the aesthetics of religion, and the observation of key events including the changing seasons, and saints' days.

Rossetti believed the Bible to be written by humans, at the inspiration of God, and that the Bible forms the basis for humans to understand their role in the world, their faith, and their relationship with God. All individuals can be assured of their place in Heaven after death. Many Victorian would have been extremely familiar with the Bible, Psalms and Prayer Book, which Rossetti references in her work. The majority of her writings in this particular selection are pre-Darwin, so she doesn't have any engagement with the conflict of science and religion.

Rossetti believed in the doctrine of soul sleep, not often discussed in modern religion. This doctrine says that after death the soul is in a kind of suspended animation – asleep, not in a "heaven" in any kind of physical or metaphorical way. The soul is instead asleep until the end of days, when it will wake and take its place in heaven.

How to apply this:

Rossetti's devotional works often include a note of doubt or questioning; the question of self-sacrifice and what it really means to be religious or a God Christian deserving of heaven. There's also the conflict of earthly and heavenly joy, with the seeming belief that one must be sacrificed to deserve the other. There is sometimes a sense of joy in her beliefs, but it's not common in this collection. Even in her non-devotional work, her religious influences are present in her use of imagery and her portrayal of characters.

ROSSETTI'S WRITING AND LITERARY INFLUENCES

Christina began writing poetry at around 12, and was first published at 18. Her first collection was *Goblin Market and Other Poems* (from which many of this selection are drawn), in 1862 when she was 31. She was critically acclaimed and popular – an unusual combination! – and compared to Elizabeth Barrett Browning, widely acknowledged at the time to be the most important female poet. However, while Browning often wrote very politically or socially motivated poetry (as well as her incredible love poetry), such as *The Cry of the Children* which is a plea to consider the pain and difficulty caused by child labour in factories, Rossetti rarely approached any political message directly in her poetry. While there are plenty of poems exploring a woman's role and place, she stops short of offering a didactic message or moral.

She wrote several collections during her life, including some specifically devotional/religious in nature, and some directed to children.

Literary influences include the Romantic movement, with poets including Shelley, Wordsworht and Keats, whose most famous quotation is perhaps "oh, for a life of sensation rather than of thought!" Romantics privilege nature and the intense beauty of emotion above all else. There's elements of this Rossetti's use of natural imagery, specifically her lyric poems like *Song* and *Birthday*. She also read a lot of Gothic literature, especially as a child, and there's some elements in this collection, such as her dead speakers in *Remember* and *Song*, and the references to darkness, blood and death.

PUBLICATION HISTORY

Goblin Market and Other Poems (1862):

Goblin Market
In the Round Tower at Jhansi
A Birthday
Remember
Maude Clare
Echo
Shut Out
Uphill
Song (When I am Dead)
No, Thank You, John
Winter: My Secret

The Prince's Progress and Other Poem (1866):
Good Friday
Twice

A Pageant and Other Poems (1881)
Soeur Louise de la Misericorde

Unpublished in lifetime:
From the Antique

CRITICAL VIEWPOINTS

Although most of the poems have their own critical viewpoints attached, there are some interesting comments below on Rossetti's body of work more generally which are useful in considering the collection as a whole.

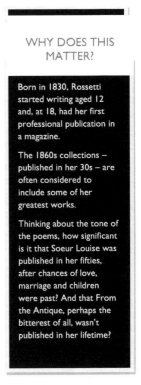

WHY DOES THIS MATTER?

Born in 1830, Rossetti started writing aged 12 and, at 18, had her first professional publication in a magazine.

The 1860s collections – published in her 30s – are often considered to include some of her greatest works.

Thinking about the tone of the poems, how significant is it that Soeur Louise was published in her fifties, after chances of love, marriage and children were past? And that From the Antique, perhaps the bitterest of all, wasn't published in her lifetime?

1877 Saturday Review (on publication of *Goblin Market and Other Poems*)

There is not much thinking in them, not much high or deep feeling, no passion and no sense of the vast blank space which a great poet always finds encompassing the ideas of life and nature and human circumstance. But they are melodious and sweet ... there is a certain quaint originality both in the versification and the concrete style in which the writer delights to treat all her fancies.

John Ruskin, in a letter to Dante Gabriel after the publication of *Goblin Market*

Your sister should exercise herself in the severest commonplace of metre until she can write as the public like.

William Michael Rossetti, in an introduction to a collection he edited after her death: I question her having ever once deliberated with herself whether or not she would write out something or other and then, after thinking about a subject, having proceeded to treat it in regular spells of work. Instead of this, something impelled her feelings or 'came into her head and her hand obeyed the dictation'.

Ford Madox Brown:
Christina Rossetti seems to us to be the most valuable poet that the Victorian Age produced

Virginia Woolf: Rossetti "starved into austere emaciation a very fine original gift, which she only wanted licence to take to itself a far finer form than, shall we say, Mrs Browning's."

Virginia Woolf (I am Christina Rossetti)
Like all instinctives you had a keen sense of the visual beauty of the world. Your poems are full of gold dust and "sweet geraniums' varied brightness"; your eye noted incessantly how rushes are "velvet-headed", and lizards have a "strange metallic mail"— your eye, indeed, observed with a sensual pre-Raphaelite intensity that must have surprised Christina the Anglo-Catholic. But to her you owed perhaps the fixity and sadness of your muse. The pressure of a tremendous faith circles and clamps together these little songs. Perhaps they owe to it their solidity. Certainly they owe to it their sadness — your God was a harsh God, your heavenly crown was set with thorns. No sooner have you feasted on beauty with your eyes than your mind tells you that beauty is vain and beauty passes. Death, oblivion, and rest lap round your songs with their dark wave. And then, incongruously, a sound of scurrying and laughter is heard. There is the patter of animals' feet and the odd guttural notes of rooks and the snufflings of obtuse furry animals grunting and nosing. For you were not a pure saint by any means. You pulled legs; you tweaked noses. You were at war with all humbug and pretence. Modest as you were, still you were drastic, sure of your gift, convinced of your vision. A firm hand pruned your lines; a sharp ear tested their music. Nothing soft, otiose, irrelevant cumbered your pages. In a word, you were an artist.

Sandra Gilbert and Susan Gubar (The Madwoman in the Attic): Rossetti loses herself in the aesthetics of renunciation, experiencing an almost extreme self-pity and self-congratulation at her self-denial. "Rossetti, banqueting on bitterness, must bury herself alive in a coffin of renunciation."

Lynda Palazzo, (Christina Rossetti's Feminist Theology, 2002):
Rossetti has radically rewritten the Fall of Eve in terms of the social and spiritual abuse of women which she sees around her and includes more than a hint that male gender oppression be interpreted as original sin.

AS-LEVEL:

The question: Using one poem as your starting point, explore how typical it is of Rossetti's themes, ideas, and techniques.

How many poems: A good rule of thumb is three plus the starting poem. You can use more – particularly if you're referring to image clusters, such as her use of door or natural imagery – but if you're using less you probably won't have enough comparison to address the 'is this characteristic' section of the question.

How to structure an answer: There are LOTS of ways to structure an essay – and you almost certainly won't be taught the same way by two different teachers. I've found this basic structure to be useful in preparing for the forty-five minute AS-Level question:

Paragraph 1 – Place the poem in Rossetti's context. What are its main themes and ideas, and how typical is this of the poetry collection? Name one or two poems connected with it, and then one or two that have significant differences. Set up an argument that you can follow – in *Twice*, Rossetti explores the duality of heavenly and earthly love. In *Goblin Market*, her conflicting attitudes to sexuality are demonstrated through the imagery of the girls but her resolution to this conflict is imperfect and unsatisfying.

Paragraph 2/3 – Exploring an aspect of language, imagery or verse form. Identify specific quotations or aspects of the poem to focus on. It might be the imagery used, or it might be structure or form. Explore the effect that this is having *in relation to the argument you established in the introduction.* Each idea here needs linking to other poems that are doing something similar, either in terms of technique or theme.

Paragraph 4 – how is this poem **uncharacteristic?** Comparing with the poems you identified in the introduction; what does she experiment with that is unusual? What is a slightly different approach in theme or language? Why do you think this is? Is it something unusual in the <u>collection</u> ("Good Friday", for example, is perhaps the most overtly religious but in Rossetti's other works is not uncommon but in this selection, it might stand out). Is it something about her age, the time the poem was written, or something else?

Paragraph 5 – a conclusion. If you had to give someone a poem that is quintessentially Rossetti – that exemplified her themes, ideas and style, would it be this one? Why /why not? Return to the argument from the introduction.

"Paragraph" is sometimes misleading; I mean a decent length, chunky paragraph. I'd be aiming to write around 2 – 2 ½ sides in the time available.

A LEVEL

Because the focus is on comparison in the A-Level essay, it's a good idea to revise the two together as soon as possible. If you study the poetry first, then as you study the play it's a good idea to link key scenes or moments with the text so that you have the two in mind together.

A five-part essay structure is still a good idea:

Introduction: Give a possible interpretation of the statement from the question, and address both texts – so, for example, Rossetti demonstrates less female power than Ibsen's Nora, in part perhaps because of their different backgrounds, but Ibsen was also far more controversial. Considering the context of both texts at the start will keep you grounded in the main assessment objectives.

Paragraph 2 / 3: Using both texts, how do you prove your argument? What supports the statement? Where are examples of it, and how are these influenced by the writers' contexts?

Paragraph 4: a counter-argument. Where do the texts challenge the statement? What about a modern audience's different viewpoint? Look for something that challenges what you're already discussing.

Conclusion: returning to the statement again, and your initial argument, evaluate the texts against one another and decide which one challenges it further, which conforms to it more.

Although AO2 isn't specifically assessed, it's essential – how else will you discuss what happens in the play or poem? A good way to think about it is that everything still needs supporting with close reference, and any discussion of AO2 can contribute to AO3 because it's discussing the context of different forms – the choices made by poet and dramatist.

TIPS FOR WRITING A COMPARATIVE ESSAY

1. **A great introduction is essential** – there needs to be a clear line of argument. It's also a good idea to include references to the key assessment objectives in the introduction, both as an indication that you're confident in all areas, and as a reminder to you of what you need to do.
2. **Use both texts side by side** – Effective comparative essays never lose sight of one of the texts, but use them both together. A simple trick to remind yourself is to include regular sentences which explain the links between the two
3. **Consider similarities AND differences** – Start with a comparison e.g. removal of individuality, then explore the different ways in which this happens.

Or start with something they both do – use of a particular symbol or idea – and then explore the different impacts of it.

4. **<u>Evaluate one versus the other, and decide which is more useful in relation to the statement</u>** Try to suggest which text is *more* in line with the statement. Or think about the different time periods; what has changed and how has this affected the different writers?

<u>Top tip!</u>
Use all the assessment objectives in the introduction. It makes sure you know **what** they are, and keeps you on track

Literary vocabulary is assessed as part of AO1 and AO2 -but the most important thing, above all else, is to be able to fully interpret the poetry's themes and ideas. The vocabulary is helpful because it can make your writing more concise and academic – but you must explore your ideas and interpretations using it, rather than simply feature-spotting.

The divides between form, structure and language are also included primarily to make sure that you cover elements of all three in your answer, supporting you in meeting all the assessment objectives.

FORM AND METRE

Form: what makes this a __poem__? The type or style of a text

Ballad		A narrative poem, usually in quatrains with an ABA rhyme scheme. Used in the oral tradition of travelling singers, lends an air of story and folktale
Dramatic monologue		A poem spoken by a persona to an unseen listener
Elegy		A poem memorialising the dead
Lyric		A poem expressing extremes of emotion, often briefly, using particularly musical language
Meter		The pattern of stressed/unstressed syllables in a line
Metrical feet	Iamb	Two syllables: Unstressed / Stressed: Da **DUM** (Often seen as the most like natural speech)
	Trochee	Two syllables: Stressed / Unstressed: **DA** dum
	Dactyl	Three syllables: Stressed / unstressed / unstressed: **DA** dum dum (often described as cantering)
	Anapest	Three syllables: Unstressed / unstressed / stressed: Da da **DUM**
Narrative		A poem telling a story
Sonnet		A fourteen line poem, using iambic pentameter (ten syllables per line in an unstressed/stressed rhythm

A set of two lines	**couplet**	A set of three lines	**triplet**
A set of four lines	**quatrain**	A set of five lines	**quintet**
A set of six lines	**sestet**	A set of seven lines	**septet**
A set of eight lines	**octet**		

STRUCTURE

*Structure: the **organization and narrative shape** of a poem.*

Anaphora	Repeating the beginning of phrases
Antithesis	A person or idea that is the direct opposite of something else.
Caesura	A break in the line, usually caused by punctuation
Collocation	Two or more words that occur together in the same order more than usually would occur, e.g. "fish and chips".
End stopped line	A sentence in poetry that finishes at the end of a line.
Enjambment	When the sentence continues over the end of a line
Hyperbaton	A change in the expected grammatical structure e.g. Some rise by sin, and some by virtue fall
Implicit responder/response	When there's an obvious, but unheard, contributor to the conversation (usually in a dramatic monologue)
Refrain	A repeated line or couplet, like a chorus
Repetition	A repeated phrase, word or image for effect
Rhyme	Two or more words sounding the same
Rhythm	The pattern of stressed/unstressed syllables in a line
Stanza	A verse or set of lines
Syndetic	Using conjunctions (and, because) to connect several clauses in a row
Syntax	The order in which the words are written.
Volta	A change of theme or idea, usually in a sonnet, at line 6 or 8

LANGUAGE

The vocabulary choices made by a writer

Alliteration	Words close together beginning with the same letter or sound
Allusion	A reference to another story or idea e.g. the Bible
Archaism	An old-fashioned phrase for the time
Assonance	Repeated vowel sounds
Dialogue	Directly quoted speech
Euphemism	A kind or pleasant way of saying something unpleasant
Exclamative	Exclamation, extremely emotive expression
Imagery	Visually descriptive or figurative language
Interrogative	Question
Imperative	Instruction or demand
Metaphor	Describing one thing as being something else
Personification	Giving inanimate objects/things human characteristics
Pronoun	Referring to a person or thing e.. you, me, this
Sibilance	Repeated "s" or "f" sounds
Simile	Comparing one thing to another using like or as
Symbol	A representation of something else.

Morning and evening
Maids heard the goblins cry:
"Come buy our orchard fruits,
Come buy, come buy:
Apples and quinces,
Lemons and oranges,
Plump unpecked cherries-
Melons and raspberries,
Bloom-down-cheeked peaches,
Swart-headed mulberries,
Wild free-born cranberries,
Crab-apples, dewberries,
Pine-apples, blackberries,
Apricots, strawberries--
All ripe together
In summer weather--
Morns that pass by,
Fair eves that fly;
Come buy, come buy;
Our grapes fresh from the vine,
Pomegranates full and fine,
Dates and sharp bullaces,
Rare pears and greengages,
Damsons and bilberries,
Taste them and try:
Currants and gooseberries,
Bright-fire-like barberries,
Figs to fill your mouth,
Citrons from the South,
Sweet to tongue and sound to eye,
Come buy, come buy."

Evening by evening
Among the brookside rushes,
Laura bowed her head to hear,

Lizzie veiled her blushes:
Crouching close together
In the cooling weather,
With clasping arms and cautioning lips,
With tingling cheeks and finger-tips.
"Lie close," Laura said,
Pricking up her golden head:
We must not look at goblin men,
We must not buy their fruits:
Who knows upon what soil they fed
Their hungry thirsty roots?"
"Come buy," call the goblins
Hobbling down the glen.
"O! cried Lizzie, Laura, Laura,
You should not peep at goblin men."
Lizzie covered up her eyes
Covered close lest they should look;
Laura reared her glossy head,
And whispered like the restless brook:
"Look, Lizzie, look, Lizzie,
Down the glen tramp little men.
One hauls a basket,
One bears a plate,
One lugs a golden dish
Of many pounds' weight.
How fair the vine must grow
Whose grapes are so luscious;
How warm the wind must blow
Through those fruit bushes."
"No," said Lizzie, "no, no, no;
Their offers should not charm us,
Their evil gifts would harm us."
She thrust a dimpled finger
In each ear, shut eyes and ran:
Curious Laura chose to linger
Wondering at each merchant man.
One had a cat's face,

One whisked a tail,
One tramped at a rat's pace,
One crawled like a snail,
One like a wombat prowled obtuse and furry,
One like a ratel tumbled hurry-scurry.
Lizzie heard a voice like voice of doves
Cooing all together:
They sounded kind and full of loves
In the pleasant weather.

Laura stretched her gleaming neck
Like a rush-imbedded swan,
Like a lily from the beck,
Like a moonlit poplar branch,
Like a vessel at the launch
When its last restraint is gone.

Backwards up the mossy glen
Turned and trooped the goblin men,
With their shrill repeated cry,
"Come buy, come buy."
When they reached where Laura was
They stood stock still upon the moss,
Leering at each other,
Brother with queer brother;
Signalling each other,
Brother with sly brother.
One set his basket down,
One reared his plate;
One began to weave a crown
Of tendrils, leaves, and rough nuts brown
(Men sell not such in any town);
One heaved the golden weight
Of dish and fruit to offer her:
"Come buy, come buy," was still their cry.
Laura stared but did not stir,
Longed but had no money:

The whisk-tailed merchant bade her taste
In tones as smooth as honey,
The cat-faced purr'd,
The rat-paced spoke a word
Of welcome, and the snail-paced even was heard;
One parrot-voiced and jolly
Cried "Pretty Goblin" still for "Pretty Polly";
One whistled like a bird.
But sweet-tooth Laura spoke in haste:
"Good folk, I have no coin;
To take were to purloin:
I have no copper in my purse,
I have no silver either,
And all my gold is on the furze
That shakes in windy weather
Above the rusty heather."
"You have much gold upon your head,"
They answered altogether:
"Buy from us with a golden curl."
She clipped a precious golden lock,
She dropped a tear more rare than pearl,
Then sucked their fruit globes fair or red:
Sweeter than honey from the rock,
Stronger than man-rejoicing wine,
Clearer than water flowed that juice;
She never tasted such before,
How should it cloy with length of use?
She sucked and sucked and sucked the more
Fruits which that unknown orchard bore,
She sucked until her lips were sore;
Then flung the emptied rinds away,
But gathered up one kernel stone,
And knew not was it night or day
As she turned home alone.

Lizzie met her at the gate
Full of wise upbraidings:

"Dear, you should not stay so late,
Twilight is not good for maidens;
Should not loiter in the glen
In the haunts of goblin men.
Do you not remember Jeanie,
How she met them in the moonlight,
Took their gifts both choice and many,
Ate their fruits and wore their flowers
Plucked from bowers
Where summer ripens at all hours?
But ever in the moonlight
She pined and pined away;
Sought them by night and day,
Found them no more, but dwindled and grew gray;
Then fell with the first snow,
While to this day no grass will grow
Where she lies low:
I planted daisies there a year ago
That never blow.
You should not loiter so."
"Nay hush," said Laura.
"Nay hush, my sister:
I ate and ate my fill,
Yet my mouth waters still;
To-morrow night I will
Buy more," and kissed her.
"Have done with sorrow;
I'll bring you plums to-morrow
Fresh on their mother twigs,
Cherries worth getting;
You cannot think what figs
My teeth have met in,
What melons, icy-cold
Piled on a dish of gold
Too huge for me to hold,
What peaches with a velvet nap,
Pellucid grapes without one seed:

Odorous indeed must be the mead
Whereon they grow, and pure the wave they drink,
With lilies at the brink,
And sugar-sweet their sap."

Golden head by golden head,
Like two pigeons in one nest
Folded in each other's wings,
They lay down, in their curtained bed:
Like two blossoms on one stem,
Like two flakes of new-fallen snow,
Like two wands of ivory
Tipped with gold for awful kings.
Moon and stars beamed in at them,
Wind sang to them lullaby,
Lumbering owls forbore to fly,
Not a bat flapped to and fro
Round their rest:
Cheek to cheek and breast to breast
Locked together in one nest.

Early in the morning
When the first cock crowed his warning,
Neat like bees, as sweet and busy,
Laura rose with Lizzie:
Fetched in honey, milked the cows,
Aired and set to rights the house,
Kneaded cakes of whitest wheat,
Cakes for dainty mouths to eat,
Next churned butter, whipped up cream,
Fed their poultry, sat and sewed;
Talked as modest maidens should
Lizzie with an open heart,
Laura in an absent dream,
One content, one sick in part;
One warbling for the mere bright day's delight,
One longing for the night.

At length slow evening came--
They went with pitchers to the reedy brook;
Lizzie most placid in her look,
Laura most like a leaping flame.
They drew the gurgling water from its deep
Lizzie plucked purple and rich golden flags,
Then turning homeward said: "The sunset flushes
Those furthest loftiest crags;
Come, Laura, not another maiden lags,
No wilful squirrel wags,
The beasts and birds are fast asleep."
But Laura loitered still among the rushes
And said the bank was steep.

And said the hour was early still,
The dew not fallen, the wind not chill:
Listening ever, but not catching
The customary cry,
"Come buy, come buy,"
With its iterated jingle
Of sugar-baited words:
Not for all her watching
Once discerning even one goblin
Racing, whisking, tumbling, hobbling;
Let alone the herds
That used to tramp along the glen,
In groups or single,
Of brisk fruit-merchant men.

Till Lizzie urged, "O Laura, come,
I hear the fruit-call, but I dare not look:
You should not loiter longer at this brook:
Come with me home.
The stars rise, the moon bends her arc,
Each glow-worm winks her spark,
Let us get home before the night grows dark;

For clouds may gather even
Though this is summer weather,
Put out the lights and drench us through;
Then if we lost our way what should we do?"

Laura turned cold as stone
To find her sister heard that cry alone,
That goblin cry,
"Come buy our fruits, come buy."
Must she then buy no more such dainty fruit?
Must she no more such succous pasture find,
Gone deaf and blind?
Her tree of life drooped from the root:
She said not one word in her heart's sore ache;
But peering thro' the dimness, naught discerning,
Trudged home, her pitcher dripping all the way;
So crept to bed, and lay
Silent 'til Lizzie slept;
Then sat up in a passionate yearning,
And gnashed her teeth for balked desire, and wept
As if her heart would break.
Day after day, night after night,
Laura kept watch in vain,
In sullen silence of exceeding pain.
She never caught again the goblin cry:
"Come buy, come buy,"
She never spied the goblin men
Hawking their fruits along the glen:
But when the noon waxed bright
Her hair grew thin and gray;
She dwindled, as the fair full moon doth turn
To swift decay, and burn
Her fire away.

One day remembering her kernel-stone
She set it by a wall that faced the south;
Dewed it with tears, hoped for a root,

Watched for a waxing shoot,
But there came none;
It never saw the sun,
It never felt the trickling moisture run:
While with sunk eyes and faded mouth
She dreamed of melons, as a traveller sees
False waves in desert drouth
With shade of leaf-crowned trees,
And burns the thirstier in the sandful breeze.

She no more swept the house,
Tended the fowls or cows,
Fetched honey, kneaded cakes of wheat,
Brought water from the brook:
But sat down listless in the chimney-nook
And would not eat.

Tender Lizzie could not bear
To watch her sister's cankerous care,
Yet not to share.
She night and morning
Caught the goblins' cry:
"Come buy our orchard fruits,
Come buy, come buy."
Beside the brook, along the glen
She heard the tramp of goblin men,
The voice and stir
Poor Laura could not hear;
Longed to buy fruit to comfort her,
But feared to pay too dear,
She thought of Jeanie in her grave,
Who should have been a bride;
But who for joys brides hope to have
Fell sick and died
In her gay prime,
In earliest winter-time,
With the first glazing rime,

With the first snow-fall of crisp winter-time.

Till Laura, dwindling,
Seemed knocking at Death's door:
Then Lizzie weighed no more
Better and worse,
But put a silver penny in her purse,
Kissed Laura, crossed the heath with clumps of furze
At twilight, halted by the brook,
And for the first time in her life
Began to listen and look.

Laughed every goblin
When they spied her peeping:
Came towards her hobbling,
Flying, running, leaping,
Puffing and blowing,
Chuckling, clapping, crowing,
Clucking and gobbling,
Mopping and mowing,
Full of airs and graces,
Pulling wry faces,
Demure grimaces,
Cat-like and rat-like,
Ratel and wombat-like,
Snail-paced in a hurry,
Parrot-voiced and whistler,
Helter-skelter, hurry-skurry,
Chattering like magpies,
Fluttering like pigeons,
Gliding like fishes, --
Hugged her and kissed her;
Squeezed and caressed her;
Stretched up their dishes,
Panniers and plates:
"Look at our apples
Russet and dun,

Bob at our cherries
Bite at our peaches,
Citrons and dates,
Grapes for the asking,
Pears red with basking
Out in the sun,
Plums on their twigs;
Pluck them and suck them,
Pomegranates, figs."

"Good folk," said Lizzie,
Mindful of Jeanie,
"Give me much and many"; --
Held out her apron,
Tossed them her penny.
"Nay, take a seat with us,
Honor and eat with us,"
They answered grinning;
"Our feast is but beginning.
Night yet is early,
Warm and dew-pearly,
Wakeful and starry:
Such fruits as these
No man can carry;
Half their bloom would fly,
Half their dew would dry,
Half their flavor would pass by.
Sit down and feast with us,
Be welcome guest with us,
Cheer you and rest with us."
"Thank you," said Lizzie; "but one waits
At home alone for me:
So, without further parleying,
If you will not sell me any
Of your fruits though much and many,
Give me back my silver penny
I tossed you for a fee."

They began to scratch their pates,
No longer wagging, purring,
But visibly demurring,
Grunting and snarling.
One called her proud,
Cross-grained, uncivil;
Their tones waxed loud,
Their looks were evil.
Lashing their tails
They trod and hustled her,
Elbowed and jostled her,
Clawed with their nails,
Barking, mewing, hissing, mocking,
Tore her gown and soiled her stocking,
Twitched her hair out by the roots,
Stamped upon her tender feet,
Held her hands and squeezed their fruits
Against her mouth to make her eat.

White and golden Lizzie stood,
Like a lily in a flood,
Like a rock of blue-veined stone
Lashed by tides obstreperously, --
Like a beacon left alone
In a hoary roaring sea,
Sending up a golden fire, --
Like a fruit-crowned orange-tree
White with blossoms honey-sweet
Sore beset by wasp and bee, --
Like a royal virgin town
Topped with gilded dome and spire
Close beleaguered by a fleet
Mad to tear her standard down.
One may lead a horse to water,
Twenty cannot make him drink.
Though the goblins cuffed and caught her,
Coaxed and fought her,

Bullied and besought her,
Scratched her, pinched her black as ink,
Kicked and knocked her,
Mauled and mocked her,
Lizzie uttered not a word;
Would not open lip from lip
Lest they should cram a mouthful in;
But laughed in heart to feel the drip
Of juice that syruped all her face,
And lodged in dimples of her chin,
And streaked her neck which quaked like curd.
At last the evil people,
Worn out by her resistance,
Flung back her penny, kicked their fruit
Along whichever road they took,
Not leaving root or stone or shoot.
Some writhed into the ground,
Some dived into the brook
With ring and ripple.
Some scudded on the gale without a sound,
Some vanished in the distance.

In a smart, ache, tingle,
Lizzie went her way;
Knew not was it night or day;
Sprang up the bank, tore through the furze,
Threaded copse and dingle,
And heard her penny jingle
Bouncing in her purse, --
Its bounce was music to her ear.
She ran and ran
As if she feared some goblin man
Dogged her with gibe or curse
Or something worse:
But not one goblin skurried after,
Nor was she pricked by fear;
The kind heart made her windy-paced

That urged her home quite out of breath with haste
And inward laughter.

She cried "Laura," up the garden,
"Did you miss me ?
Come and kiss me.
Never mind my bruises,
Hug me, kiss me, suck my juices
Squeezed from goblin fruits for you,
Goblin pulp and goblin dew.
Eat me, drink me, love me;
Laura, make much of me:
For your sake I have braved the glen
And had to do with goblin merchant men."

Laura started from her chair,
Flung her arms up in the air,
Clutched her hair:
"Lizzie, Lizzie, have you tasted
For my sake the fruit forbidden?
Must your light like mine be hidden,
Your young life like mine be wasted,
Undone in mine undoing,
And ruined in my ruin;
Thirsty, cankered, goblin-ridden?"
She clung about her sister,
Kissed and kissed and kissed her:
Tears once again
Refreshed her shrunken eyes,
Dropping like rain
After long sultry drouth;
Shaking with aguish fear, and pain,
She kissed and kissed her with a hungry mouth.

Her lips began to scorch,
That juice was wormwood to her tongue,
She loathed the feast:

Writhing as one possessed she leaped and sung,
Rent all her robe, and wrung
Her hands in lamentable haste,
And beat her breast.
Her locks streamed like the torch
Borne by a racer at full speed,
Or like the mane of horses in their flight,
Or like an eagle when she stems the light
Straight toward the sun,
Or like a caged thing freed,
Or like a flying flag when armies run.

Swift fire spread through her veins, knocked at her heart,

Met the fire smouldering there
And overbore its lesser flame,
She gorged on bitterness without a name:
Ah! fool, to choose such part
Of soul-consuming care!
Sense failed in the mortal strife:
Like the watch-tower of a town
Which an earthquake shatters down,
Like a lightning-stricken mast,
Like a wind-uprooted tree
Spun about,
Like a foam-topped water-spout
Cast down headlong in the sea,
She fell at last;
Pleasure past and anguish past,
Is it death or is it life?

Life out of death.
That night long Lizzie watched by her,
Counted her pulse's flagging stir,
Felt for her breath,
Held water to her lips, and cooled her face
With tears and fanning leaves:

But when the first birds chirped about their eaves,
And early reapers plodded to the place
Of golden sheaves,
And dew-wet grass
Bowed in the morning winds so brisk to pass,
And new buds with new day
Opened of cup-like lilies on the stream,
Laura awoke as from a dream,
Laughed in the innocent old way,
Hugged Lizzie but not twice or thrice;
Her gleaming locks showed not one thread of grey,
Her breath was sweet as May,
And light danced in her eyes.

Days, weeks, months, years
Afterwards, when both were wives
With children of their own;
Their mother-hearts beset with fears,
Their lives bound up in tender lives;
Laura would call the little ones
And tell them of her early prime,
Those pleasant days long gone
Of not-returning time:
Would talk about the haunted glen,
The wicked, quaint fruit-merchant men,
Their fruits like honey to the throat,
But poison in the blood;
(Men sell not such in any town;)
Would tell them how her sister stood
In deadly peril to do her good,
And win the fiery antidote:
Then joining hands to little hands
Would bid them cling together,
"For there is no friend like a sister,
In calm or stormy weather,
To cheer one on the tedious way,
To fetch one if one goes astray,

To lift one if one totters down,
To strengthen whilst one stands."

Discuss Rossetti's presentation of the afterlife in *Echo*.

In your answer explore the author's use of language, imagery and verse form, and consider ways in which you find the poem characteristic of Rossetti's work in your selection.

Come to me in the silence of the night;
Come in the speaking silence of a dream;
Come with soft rounded cheeks and eyes as bright
As sunlight on a stream;
Come back in tears,
O memory, hope, love of finished years.

O dream how sweet, too sweet, too bitter sweet,
Whose wakening should have been in Paradise,
Where souls brimfull of love abide and meet;
Where thirsting longing eyes
Watch the slow door
That opening, letting in, lets out no more.

Yet come to me in dreams, that I may live
My very life again though cold in death:
Come back to me in dreams, that I may give
Pulse for pulse, breath for breath:
Speak low, lean low
As long ago, my love, how long ago.

Discuss Rossetti's presentation of desire in Soeur Louise de la Misericorde

In your answer explore the author's use of language, imagery and verse form, and consider ways in which you find the poem characteristic of Rossetti's work in your selection.

I have desired, and I have been desired;
But now the days are over of desire,
Now dust and dying embers mock my fire;
Where is the hire for which my life was hired?
Oh vanity of vanities, desire!

Longing and love, pangs of a perished pleasure,
Longing and love, a disenkindled fire,
And memory a bottomless gulf of mire,
And love a fount of tears outrunning measure;
Oh vanity of vanities, desire!

Now from my heart, love's deathbed, trickles, trickles,
Drop by drop slowly, drop by drop of fire,
The dross of life, of love, of spent desire;
Alas, my rose of life gone all to prickles,--
Oh vanity of vanities, desire!

Oh vanity of vanities, desire;
Stunting my hope which might have strained up higher,
Turning my garden plot to barren mire;
Oh death-struck love, oh disenkindled fire,
Oh vanity of vanities, desire!

Discuss Rossetti's presentation of the despair in *In the Round Tower at Jhansi*

In your answer explore the author's use of language, imagery and verse form, and consider ways in which you find the poem characteristic of Rossetti's work in your selection.

A hundred, a thousand to one: even so;
Not a hope in the world remained:
The swarming howling wretches below
 Gained and gained and gained.

Skene looked at his pale young wife.   5
Is the time come?'—'The time is come.'
Young, strong, and so full of life,
The agony struck them dumb.

Close his arm about her now,
Close her cheek to his,   10
Close the pistol to her brow—
God forgive them this!

'Will it hurt much?' 'No, mine own:
I wish I could bear the pang for both.'—
'I wish I could bear the pang alone: 15
Courage, dear, I am not loth.'

Kiss and kiss: 'It is not pain
Thus to kiss and die.
One kiss more.'—'And yet one again.'—
'Good-bye.'—'Good-bye.'   20

Discuss Rossetti's presentation of nature in *Birthday*

In your answer explore the author's use of language, imagery and verse form, and consider ways in which you find the poem characteristic of Rossetti's work in your selection.

> My heart is like a singing bird
> Whose nest is in a watered shoot;
> My heart is like an apple-tree
> Whose boughs are bent with thickset fruit;
> My heart is like a rainbow shell
> That paddles in a halcyon sea;
> My heart is gladder than all these
> Because my love is come to me.
>
> Raise me a dais of silk and down;
> Hang it with vair* and purple dyes;
> Carve it in doves and pomegranates,
> And peacocks with a hundred eyes;
> Work it in gold and silver grapes,
> In leaves and silver fleurs-de-lys;
> Because the birthday of my life
> Is come, my love is come to me

*Vair — decorative furs.

Discuss Rossetti's presentation of male and female relationships in *Maude Clare*

In your answer explore the author's use of language, imagery and verse form, and consider ways in which you find the poem characteristic of Rossetti's work in your selection.

Out of the church she followed them
With a lofty step and mien:
His bride was like a village maid,
Maude Clare was like a queen.

"Son Thomas, " his lady mother said,
With smiles, almost with tears:
"May Nell and you but live as true
As we have done for years;

"Your father thirty years ago
Had just your tale to tell;
But he was not so pale as you,
Nor I so pale as Nell."

My lord was pale with inward strife,
And Nell was pale with pride;
My lord gazed long on pale Maude Clare
Or ever he kissed the bride.

"Lo, I have brought my gift, my lord,
Have brought my gift, " she said:
To bless the hearth, to bless the board,
To bless the marriage-bed.

"Here's my half of the golden chain
You wore about your neck,
That day we waded ankle-deep
For lilies in the beck:

"Here's my half of the faded leaves
We plucked from the budding bough,
With feet amongst the lily leaves, -
The lilies are budding now."

He strove to match her scorn with scorn,
He faltered in his place:
"Lady, " he said, - "Maude Clare, " he said-
"Maude Clare, " – and hid his face.

She turn'd to Nell: "My Lady Nell,
I have a gift for you;
Though, were it fruit, the blooms were gone,
Or, were it flowers, the dew.

"Take my share of a fickle heart,
Mine of a paltry love:
Take it or leave it as you will,
I wash my hands thereof."

"And what you leave, " said Nell, "I'll take,
And what you spurn, I'll wear;
For he's my lord for better and worse,
And him I love Maude Clare.

"Yea, though you're taller by the head,
More wise and much more fair:
I'll love him till he loves me best,
Me best of all Maude Clare.

Discuss Rossetti's presentation of religious doubt and faith in *Good Friday*

In your answer explore the author's use of language, imagery and verse form, and consider ways in which you find the poem characteristic of Rossetti's work in your selection.

> Am I a stone, and not a sheep,
> That I can stand, O Christ, beneath Thy cross,
> To number drop by drop Thy blood's slow loss,
> And yet not weep?
>
> Not so those women loved
> Who with exceeding grief lamented Thee;
> Not so fallen Peter weeping bitterly;
> Not so the thief was moved;
>
> Not so the Sun and Moon
> Which hid their faces in a starless sky,
> A horror of great darkness at broad noon—
> I, only I.
>
> Yet give not o'er,
> But seek Thy sheep, true Shepherd of the flock;
> Greater than Moses, turn and look once more
> And smite a rock.

Section 2 – Drama and Poetry pre-1900

Answer **one** question from this section. You should spend about 1 hour and 15 minutes on this section.

In your answer, you should refer to one drama text and one poetry text from the following lists:

Drama	Poetry
Christopher Marlowe: *Edward II*	Geoffrey Chaucer: *The Merchant's Prologue and Tale*
John Webster: *The Duchess of Malfi*	John Milton: *Paradise Lost Books 9 & 10*
Oliver Goldsmith: *She Stoops to Conquer*	Samuel Taylor Coleridge: *Selected Poems*
Henrik Ibsen: *A Doll's House*	Alfred, Lord Tennyson: *Maud*
Oscar Wilde: *An Ideal Husband*	Christina Rossetti: *Selected Poems*

Love is invariably possessive.

In light of this view, consider ways in which writers explore love and possession.

Good writing about sexual relationships is invariably moral.

In light of this view, consider ways in which wrtiers explore the morality of sexual relationships.

Men may seem to be more powerful than women but the reality is very different

In light of this view, consider ways in which writers explore power and gender.

Forbidden tastes are sweetest.

In light fo this view, consider ways in which wrtiers explore the atteraction of that which is forbidden.

Conflict in literature generally arises from misundertanding.

In light of this view, consider ways in which writers make use of misunderstanding.

Rank and social status are enemies of happiness.

In light of this view, consider ways in which writers explore the effects of rank and social status.

Answer **one** question from this section. You should spend about 1 hour and 15 minutes on this section.

In your answer, you should refer to one drama text and one poetry text from the following lists:

Drama	Poetry
Christopher Marlowe: *Edward II* John Webster: *The Duchess of Malfi* Oliver Goldsmith: *She Stoops to Conquer* Henrik Ibsen: *A Doll's House* Oscar Wilde: *An Ideal Husband*	Geoffrey Chaucer: *The Merchant's Prologue and Tale* John Milton: *Paradise Lost Books 9 & 10* Samuel Taylor Coleridge: *Selected Poems* Alfred, Lord Tennyson: *Maud* Christina Rossetti: *Selected Poems*

Endings are always, in some sense, artificial.'
In the light of this view, consider ways in which writers conclude their work.

'What can male writers know or understand about women?'
In the light of this view, consider ways in which writers present women.

'Arrogance is the most monstrous of faults.'
In the light of this view, consider ways in which writers portray arrogance.

'It is rarely good for us to get what we want.'
In the light of this view, consider ways in which writers portray appetites and desires, and their consequences.

'Wrongdoing and villainy can provoke both admiration and disgust at the same time.'
In the light of this view, consider ways in which writers present wrongdoing and villainy.

'Seduction is most effectively accomplished through flattery.'
In the light of this view, consider ways in which writers represent seduction.

Answer **one** question from this section. You should spend about 1 hour and 15 minutes on this section.

In your answer, you should refer to one drama text and one poetry text from the following lists:

Drama	Poetry
Christopher Marlowe: *Edward II*	Geoffrey Chaucer: *The Merchant's Prologue and Tale*
John Webster: *The Duchess of Malfi*	John Milton: *Paradise Lost Books 9 & 10*
Oliver Goldsmith: *She Stoops to Conquer*	Samuel Taylor Coleridge: *Selected Poems*
Henrik Ibsen: *A Doll's House*	Alfred, Lord Tennyson: *Maud*
Oscar Wilde: *An Ideal Husband*	Christina Rossetti: *Selected Poems*

To embrace love is to embrace danger
In the light of this view, consider writers' treatment of love

Literature explores the conflict between order and chaos
In the light of this view, consider ways in which writers represent order and chaos.

The fascination of innocence lies in its fragility

In the light of this view, consider ways in which writers represent innocence.

Verbal wit is women's strongest weapon
In the light of this view, consider ways in which writers represent women's use of language.

Court, city or country: a writer's choice of setting is always signiciant
In the light of this view, discuss ways in which writers use settings.

Great literary characters are always putting on a show
In the light of this view, consider ways in which writers present literary characters.

Answer **one** question from this section. You should spend about 1 hour and 15 minutes on this section.

In your answer, you should refer to one drama text and one poetry text from the following lists:

Drama	Poetry
Christopher Marlowe: *Edward II* John Webster: *The Duchess of Malfi* Oliver Goldsmith: *She Stoops to Conquer* Henrik Ibsen: *A Doll's House* Oscar Wilde: *An Ideal Husband*	Geoffrey Chaucer: *The Merchant's Prologue and Tale* John Milton: *Paradise Lost Books 9 & 10* Samuel Taylor Coleridge: *Selected Poems* Alfred, Lord Tennyson: *Maud* Christina Rossetti: *Selected Poems*

Literature rarely shows power being used well

In the light of this view, consider ways in which writers present the use of power.

Experience all too often leads to disillusionment

In the light of this view, consider ways in which writers explore the consequences of experience.

Good writing must, above all, help us to view the world afresh.

In the light of this view, consider ways in which writers help us to see the world in new ways.

Literature shows us that sexual desire must be restrained

In the light of this view, consider ways in which writers present sexual desire.

Humour helps us come to terms with human weakness

In the light of this view, consider ways in which writers explore human weaknesses.

Writers, readers and audiences delight in the spectacle of sinfulness

In the light of this view, consider ways in which writers present sin.

Answer **one** question from this section. You should spend about 1 hour and 15 minutes on this section.

In your answer, you should refer to one drama text and one poetry text from the following lists:

Drama	Poetry
Christopher Marlowe: *Edward II*	Geoffrey Chaucer: *The Merchant's Prologue and Tale*
John Webster: *The Duchess of Malfi*	John Milton: *Paradise Lost Books 9 & 10*
Oliver Goldsmith: *She Stoops to Conquer*	Samuel Taylor Coleridge: *Selected Poems*
Henrik Ibsen: *A Doll's House*	Alfred, Lord Tennyson: *Maud*
Oscar Wilde: *An Ideal Husband*	Christina Rossetti: *Selected Poems*

Pride goes before a fall: the greater the pride, the harder the fall
In the light of this view, consider ways in which writers present pride and its consequences.

Love is a kind of madness
In the light of this view, consider ways in which writers portray love and its effects.

In literature the use of time is always significant
In the light of this view, consider ways in which writers make use of time.

Words can entice use, can compel us, can ensnare us
In the light of this view, consider ways in which writers present persuasive or seductive uses of language

We admire defiance and idsobedience – especially in the face of the inevitable
In the light of this view, consider ways in which writers explore defiance and disobedience

There is a fine line between heroism and foolishness
In the light of this view, consider ways in which writers explore heroism.

Answer **one** question from this section. You should spend about 1 hour and 15 minutes on this section.

In your answer, you should refer to one drama text and one poetry text from the following lists:

Drama	Poetry
Christopher Marlowe: *Edward II* John Webster: *The Duchess of Malfi* Oliver Goldsmith: *She Stoops to Conquer* Henrik Ibsen: *A Doll's House* Oscar Wilde: *An Ideal Husband*	Geoffrey Chaucer: *The Merchant's Prologue and Tale* John Milton: *Paradise Lost Books 9 & 10* Samuel Taylor Coleridge: *Selected Poems* Alfred, Lord Tennyson: *Maud* Christina Rossetti: *Selected Poems*

Because we know we must die, we live all the more intensely.
In the light of this view, consider ways in which writers portray the idea of living life to the full.

Laughter is always dangerous
In the light of this view, discuss ways in which writers use humour.

Love is the most selfish of emotions
In the light of this view, discuss ways in which writers explore love.

Appetite – whether for power, knowledge, sex or money – is a destructive force.
In the light of this view, discuss ways in which writers explore appetites.

Happiness – a state to which all aspire but which few will ever reach.
In the light of this view, discuss ways in which writers explore the search for happiness.

Irony exposes the gap between the way things appear to be and the way they are.
In the light of this view, discuss ways in which writers use irony.

Answer **one** question from this section. You should spend about 1 hour and 15 minutes on this section.

In your answer, you should refer to one drama text and one poetry text from the following lists:

Drama	Poetry
Christopher Marlowe: *Edward II*	Geoffrey Chaucer: *The Merchant's Prologue and Tale*
John Webster: *The Duchess of Malfi*	John Milton: *Paradise Lost Books 9 & 10*
Oliver Goldsmith: *She Stoops to Conquer*	Samuel Taylor Coleridge: *Selected Poems*
Henrik Ibsen: *A Doll's House*	Alfred, Lord Tennyson: *Maud*
Oscar Wilde: *An Ideal Husband*	Christina Rossetti: *Selected Poems*

Love is a restless emotion, driving growth and change.

In the light of this view, discuss ways in which writers explore the power and effects of love.

Life is a game of chance in which skilful players risk everything.

In the light of this view, discuss ways in which writers explore risk and chance

Temptation arises from a willingness to be tempted.

In the light of this view, discuss ways in which writers explore temptation and its consequences.

There is a tension between the attractiveness of wrongdoing and fear of its consequences.

In the light of this view, discuss ways in which writers explore aspects of wrongdoing.

For women, sex is a means to an end. For men, it is an end in itself.

In the light of this view, discuss ways in which writers explore differing attitudes to sex.

It is the processes of argument and persuasion which most strongly engage us.

In the light of this view, discuss ways in which writers use argument and persuasion.

Answer **one** question from this section. You should spend about 1 hour and 15 minutes on this section.

In your answer, you should refer to one drama text and one poetry text from the following lists:

Drama	Poetry
Christopher Marlowe: *Edward II* John Webster: *The Duchess of Malfi* Oliver Goldsmith: *She Stoops to Conquer* Henrik Ibsen: *A Doll's House* Oscar Wilde: *An Ideal Husband*	Geoffrey Chaucer: *The Merchant's Prologue and Tale* John Milton: *Paradise Lost Books 9 & 10* Samuel Taylor Coleridge: *Selected Poems* Alfred, Lord Tennyson: *Maud* Christina Rossetti: *Selected Poems*

The struggle with God is all consuming and passionate.

In the light of this view, discuss ways in which writers explore relationships with God.

It is their weaknesses which make heroic characters interesting.

In the light of this view, discuss ways in which writers present heroic characters.

Pride is inescapable from foolishness

In the light of this view, discuss ways in which writers present the nature of pride.

Evil characters are lonely characters and their isolations fascinates us.

In the light of this view, discuss ways in which writers explore the nature of evil.

Desire dazzles and destroys people like light in a candle flame.

In the light of this view, discuss ways in which writers present intense desire and their consequences.

Women are the subtler sex; more varied in their attractions, more ingenious in their stratagems.

In the light of this view, discuss ways in which writers present women.

Answer **one** question from this section. You should spend about 1 hour and 15 minutes on this section.

In your answer, you should refer to one drama text and one poetry text from the following lists:

Drama	Poetry
Christopher Marlowe: *Edward II*	Geoffrey Chaucer: *The Merchant's Prologue and Tale*
John Webster: *The Duchess of Malfi*	John Milton: *Paradise Lost Books 9 & 10*
Oliver Goldsmith: *She Stoops to Conquer*	Samuel Taylor Coleridge: *Selected Poems*
Henrik Ibsen: *A Doll's House*	Alfred, Lord Tennyson: *Maud*
Oscar Wilde: *An Ideal Husband*	Christina Rossetti: *Selected Poems*

Masks, poses, facades, deception – all are weapons in the battle of life.

In the light of this view, discuss ways in which writers present disguise and deception.

In literature, the main purpose of setting is to intensify the presentation of character.

In the light of this view, discuss the effects writers create by their use of settings.

We are both fascinated and repelled by the obsessions of others.

In the light of this view, discuss ways in which writers present obsession and its effects.

Flawed characters are always more memorable than any moral lessons that literature seeks to draw from them.

In the light of this view, discuss ways in which writers present characters' flaws and failings.

Of all the emotions that drive us, fear is the strongest.

In the light of this view, discuss ways in which writers present the power of fear.

The more intense the passion, the more bitter its effects

In the light of this view, discuss ways in which writers present intense emotions.

135

Answer **one** question from this section. You should spend about 1 hour and 15 minutes on this section.

In your answer, you should refer to one drama text and one poetry text from the following lists:

Drama	Poetry
Christopher Marlowe: *Edward II* John Webster: *The Duchess of Malfi* Oliver Goldsmith: *She Stoops to Conquer* Henrik Ibsen: *A Doll's House* Oscar Wilde: *An Ideal Husband*	Geoffrey Chaucer: *The Merchant's Prologue and Tale* John Milton: *Paradise Lost Books 9 & 10* Samuel Taylor Coleridge: *Selected Poems* Alfred, Lord Tennyson: *Maud* Christina Rossetti: *Selected Poems*

The pleasures of pursuit are greater than the thrill of conquest.

In the light of this view, discuss ways in which writers present seduction and its consequences.

Vanity drives us and can all too easily destroy us.

In the light of this view, discuss ways in which writers present the power of vanity

By inviting us to laugh at foolishness writers encourage us to laugh at ourselves.

In the light of this view, discuss ways in which writers use mockery and humour.

Conflict in literature generally arises from misundertanding.

In light of this view, consider ways in which writers make use of misunderstanding.

Experience all too often leads to disillusionment

In the light of this view, consider ways in which writers explore the consequences of experience.

Court, city or country: a writer's choice of setting is always signiciant

In the light of this view, discuss ways in which writers use settings.

Thanks for reading! I hope you've found this guide useful, and interesting. If so you could have a look at my website – www.charlotteunsworth.com – or have a look at my author page on Amazon: https://www.amazon.co.uk/-/e/B00BCP1HC2

Printed in Great Britain
by Amazon